Contents

Repairing Broken Walls

Repairing Broken Walls

RESTORING JOY & PEACE

Sandra Lott

Your New Life Ministries LLC

Published by: Your New Life Ministries LLC
Third Edition

www.yournewlifeministries.org

Published in the United States of America by
Your New Life Ministries
LLC

I would like to thank the Lord, through His patience with me and the help of the Holy Spirit, He led me through my own restoration. Overcoming years of my own broken heart and spirit, the Lord led me little by little removing the rubble, and exchanging the ashes within my heart with the joy and beauty of his Spirit.

I thank Him and praise Him every day for the journey He has led me on and the gift He has placed within me to help others overcome their own broken heart.

"Your people will rebuild the ancient ruins and will raise up the age-old foundations; you will be called Repairer of Broken Walls, Restorer of Streets with Dwellings." Isaiah 58:12

Forward

In Repairing Broken Walls, Sandra Lott presents the principles of Scripture that helped her repair and heal her own broken heart. Sandra, a former victim of abuse, has risen above the brokenness, and has built a life on the foundation of Jesus Christ as her Savior and Lord!

In this book, spiritual parallels are drawn between the principles found in the book of Nehemiah, and reestablishing our lives after devastation, and captivity, facing the mess, and restoring our walls of defense one brick at a time. Sandra shows you how to move beyond the rocks, the rubbish, and relics of a past life, and restore the boundaries and the beauty of better times, even helping others to heal. Repairing Broken Walls isn't a self-help book but relies heavily on the Scriptures, the Gospel, and the Spirit to reclaim what the enemy has taken away, nor is it an easy-fix approach. It calls on us to restore our walls while resisting a real enemy who wants to defeat us.

You wouldn't be reading this book if you didn't have a real desire to repair your broken places. I pray God will use the truths presented in this book to restore you and give you a hope and a future.

Pastor Jim Patterson

Introduction

In dealing with my own broken heart, I began searching for the love of God to heal all that was broken inside me and fill in all the cracks, and make me whole again. This book comes from my own experience. I was so broken my spirit was crushed within me. I needed to feel as if there was a reason for me being here and that I wasn't placed here to be everyone's punching bag. I needed to feel valued and loved.

If you are reading this book and are in search of the Lord's pathway to healing, I pray that God will open your eyes and your heart to receive a word from Him. Discover how God wants to restore all that is broken within you as you travel through the books of Nehemiah and Ezra with me. Learn from them as they rebuilt the temple and the wall of Jerusalem after the exile and apply it to your own broken heart.

A broken heart and spirit will blind you to what is right in front of you. It will blind you to the truth. I was sure that I was on the right path, and my heart was right before God until He showed me little by little, as He healed me that I had a long way to go. I discovered just how broken my heart really was as I began to realize all the bitterness, resentment and fear I had inside. You react by how you perceive things to be, and if your heart is broken, it will cloud your mind and your thinking. Your perception will be wrong and how you react will be as well. At the direction of a dear sister in the Lord, I learned to step back and question my actions and why I reacted and responded the way I did. I began seeing the heartache I had inside and what it was doing to me. I knew that my spiritual growth was slow, and now I knew why. If you keep reacting the same way and getting the same results, don't expect to keep reacting that way and be different—it will not happen. I was searching for something that I already had and did not know it. God loves everyone, and the moment we ask Jesus into our hearts, we have his love in our hearts as well.

"I have loved you with an everlasting love; I have drawn you with loving-kindness" *(Jeremiah 31:3)*

3

His love has been with me all along, and it has been with you as well since the moment you were born again. Satan tries to distort and conceal the truth of God's love by overwhelming us with heartache and problems. God wants to reveal the truth.

The change did not happen all at once for me, and the depth of my heartache became clearer and clearer as my eyes opened more and more to the truth of my condition. Someone would say something or ask me something, and in my messed up state, I would take it all wrong. I would take it as "Someone is trying to use me again." I would react and say something rash and then step back in surprise at my own words and wonder where that came from—"Out of the overflow of the heart, the mouth speaks." The Holy Spirit would gently make me aware that it came from within the cracked walls of my heart—a heart that needed much repair.

Through a prayer ministry at the church I had been attending, they had taught me that I needed to go back to the first place where I ever felt pain. They emphasized that if I had trouble remembering or my heart was too scared to revisit it, I would go to the Lord in prayer, and the Holy Spirit would help. They told me that it might be a process depending on the amount of pain I had endured and how deep the heartache went and how many events had caused it.

I used what they taught me and continued the process of getting alone with God and praying and allowing Him to reveal the issues within my heart. The amount of pain I had locked away took several years. Each person is different, and part of my trouble was the need to separate myself from the one inflicting the pain. Then the Lord began the healing process. I had to go back to each instance and pray and release. I had to release it, forgive, and give it to God. He cannot take what you will not give Him. If you want Him to replace the pain with joy, then you need to give it to Him. You cannot hold anything back either; it is not easy, but it is necessary. You cannot tell a doctor treating an infection, like a wound or boil with a lot of pus inside to only clean out part of it. He needs to clean it all out in order for it to heal. You must give it all over to God, and that means you cannot hold on to any bitter feelings, unforgiving ways, anger, or resentment.

You must forgive all involved including yourself. Without forgiveness, the healing cannot take place. "Therefore if you are offering your gift at the altar and there remember that your brother or sister has something against you, leave your gift there in front of the altar. First, go and be reconciled to them; then come and offer your gift." (Matthew 5:23–24)

Forgiveness must reign in your heart; after all, who are we not to forgive when Jesus died so that we may receive it? Leaving any amount of bitterness in your heart only creates an open door for the enemy to keep control over your life. Hasn't He given you enough heartache without inviting more? Let go and forgive. God will take care of those who hurt you. "For if you forgive other people when they sin against you, your heavenly Father will also forgive you. But if you do not forgive others their sins your Father will not forgive your sins." (Matthew 6:14–15)

You must release all your pain and everyone who hurt you to God. How can He take and repair and heal what you will not give Him? The most important part of healing your heart is allowing God to, first of all, get rid of the darkness within it. Pain, lack of forgiveness, bitterness, etc. is darkness, and it is what is destroying your heart and keeping it broken and cracked—not yielding any fruit. I was more deeply wounded than I thought. I would give something over to God and feel wonderful and almost normal then something else would surface.

I realized that for me, this might not be the situation for everyone, but for me, the healing process might take a while. I was determined to keep going and not give up. I saw giving up as giving Satan the upper hand, and he wreaked enough havoc in my life, and I was not about to let Him have any more of it.

Jesus said we have victory through Him, and I was determined to receive it. I was determined to see the process through no matter what came my way and no matter what new attack Satan would try. I was going to see this through until God completely healed my heart.

I urge you to do the same, and if you are feeling shaky in the faith area and weak, then go to God in prayer and ask for his help. Ask Him to give you the strength to see this through. "My grace is sufficient for you, for My power is made perfect in weakness. Therefore, I will boast all the more gladly about my weaknesses so that Christ's power may rest on me. That is why—for Christ's sake—I delight in weaknesses, in insults, in hardships, in persecutions, in difficulties. For when I am weak, then I am strong."
   (2 Corinthians 12:8–10)

My heart is completely healed, and as long as you see this through and do not give up on God, He will be faithful to heal your heart as well.

"The righteous cry out, and the Lord hears them; He delivers them from all their troubles. The Lord is close to the brokenhearted and saves those who are crushed in spirit. The righteous person may have many troubles, but the Lord delivers Him from them all; He protects all his bones, not one of them will be broken." (Psalms 34:17–20)

Part 1: Ancient Ruins

"Your people will rebuild the ancient ruins."

1

⌇⌇

Residue Of The Past

In part 1 of this book, we are going to deal with the ancient ruins, where the pain began. Chapter 1: "Residue of the Past" will deal with examining your heart and admitting to the emotional issues you have to begin the process of releasing them. In chapter 2: "Discovering the Cracks" takes you on a journey back to the first place you felt pain— the first place your heart was broken.

The definition of ancient is the "Remains of something destroyed; waste places; desolation." It has several Hebrew origins. One is olam meaning, "Forever, continual, days of old, eternal and everlasting." Another one is redeem meaning, "before time." God's love is everlasting, continual, and without end; and He wants to remove the pain and fill your heart with his eternal love, peace, and joy.

A broken heart is the result of past events. Something or someone in the past did something or said something that broke your heart. When severely broken, it is the result of being hurt over and over. The pain you endured can have lasting effects and leave a residue made up of insecurity, fear, bitterness, the inability to forgive, depression, despair, self-pity, and hopelessness. "O God, the nations have invaded your inheritance; they have defiled your holy temple, they have reduced Jerusalem to rubble. They have left the dead bodies of your servants as food for the birds of the sky, the flesh of your own people for the animals of the wild" (Psalms 79:1–2).

Ancient ruins tell of something that once was and is now in ruins, and in dealing with your heart, it was at one time healthy, whole, and happy. God is the ancient of days. "Yes, and from ancient days I am He. No one can deliver out of my hand. When I act, who can reverse it?" (Isaiah 43:13). He wants to heal your heart and make you whole again as "before time," before your heart was broken. "They will rebuild the ancient ruins and restore the places long devastated; they will renew the ruined cities that have been devastated for generations." (Isaiah 61:4)

Looking into the gates of Jerusalem and the walls that were torn down, you can see the symbolism behind them. They point to Jesus Christ, our broken relationship with Him, and broken hearts that we come to Him to repair. The walls were torn down when the Babylonians captured the Israelites, and they were sent into exile. There are no walls of protection to the unsaved soul and to the one who is saved and sins against God. The Israelites, in entering the Promised Land, did not get rid of all the Canaanites, as the Lord told them, and they proved to be a thorn in their side. When we are saved, we are to leave our old life behind, and we are not to hold on to any part of it. "You were taught, with regard to your former way of life, to put off your old self, which is being corrupted by its deceitful desires; to be made new in the attitude of your minds; and to put on the new self, created to be like God in true righteousness and holiness" (Ephesians 4:22–24).

It will drag you back into a life of sin otherwise. "Do not be misled, 'Bad company corrupts good character'" (1 Corinthians 15:33). This is what happened to the Israelites. They started to intermarry, and along with that, some of the idol worship of the Canaanites worked their way in through the Israelites. Consequences would happen due to their sin, and they would cry out to God, and He would deliver them until the cycle would happen all over again.

The book of Nehemiah is about being saved and the Lord putting his wall of protection around your heart and soul and your life. It is also about the one who backslides and falls into sin and the repentance that comes when the penalty is too much. The book of Nehemiah is symbolic of the broken relationship between God and humanity that originated in the Garden of Eden and was restored and reconciled to God through Jesus Christ. "Once you were alienated from God and were enemies in your minds because of your evil behavior. But now He has reconciled you by Christ's physical body through death to present you holy in his sight, without blemish and free from accusation—if you continue in your faith, established and firm, and do not move from the hope held out in the gospel. This is the gospel that you heard and that has been proclaimed to every creature under heaven, and of which I, Paul, have become a servant" (Colossians 1:21–23).

Nehemiah is about God repairing the walls torn down due to sin and also about repairing the walls due to a broken heart. Nehemiah and the gates and walls of Jerusalem are about restoration and healing. It was God and his mercy and love who placed a burden in Nehemiah's heart to repair the wall of Jerusalem and the temple through the overseeing of Ezra. "I had not told anyone what my God had put in my heart to do for Jerusalem" (Nehemiah 2:12). In any of the situations above, when we cry out to God with a sincere heart, He will hear and answer us. "God is our refuge and strength and ever-present help in times of trouble" (Psalms 46:1). "The name of the Lord is a strong tower; the righteous run to it and are safe." (Proverbs 18:10)

Then we use our sword with one hand always being ready to protect our heart from the attacks of the enemy as was the case with Nehemiah. Sanballat, who represented the enemy, kept trying to ruin Nehemiah's attempt to repair the walls. Nehemiah and the rest of the people working to repair the walls had to be prepared. They kept a sword in one hand, and one would sound the trumpets to notify the rest. Our mouth is our trumpet cry to God, and our sword is the Bible.

"For the Word of God is living and active. Sharper than any double-edged sword, it penetrates even to dividing soul and spirit, joints and marrow; it judges the thoughts and attitudes of the heart." (Hebrews 4:12) "The tongue has the power of life and death, and those who love it will eat its fruit." (Proverbs 18:21)

They worked with one hand and held their sword with the other. We must speak the Word in faith—faith comes by hearing, and it puts it into action when we speak it, and then we must continue to hold onto the Word and stand on it. "For you have exalted above all things your Name and your Word" (Psalms 138:2). God is faithful to perform his Word. "The one who calls you is faithful and He will do it." (1 Thess. 5:24)

When we continue to confess the Word and believe it at all times in good and in bad, persevering in faith, we will grow into maturity and be promoted to where God wants us to be. "Blessed is the man who perseveres under trial because when He has stood the test, He will receive the crown of life that God has promised to those who love Him." (James 1:12)

Holding on to your faith is not easy, but if you do you will receive your promised reward, your answered prayers. "So do not throw away your confidence; it will be richly rewarded. You need to persevere so that when you have done the will of God, you will receive what He has promised. For in just a very little while, 'He who is coming will come and will not delay. But My righteous one will live by faith. And if He shrinks back, I will not be pleased with Him.' But we are not of those who shrink back and are destroyed, but of those who believe and are saved." (Hebrews 10:35–39)

"Brothers, as an example of patience in the face of suffering, take the

prophets who spoke in the name of the Lord. As you know, we consider blessed those who have persevered. You have heard of Job's perseverance and have seen what the Lord finally brought about. The Lord is full of compassion and mercy." (James 5:10–11)

Whenever God wants to repair or restore something or someone, He will put a burden on the hearts of those He intends to use. "In the first year of Cyrus king of Persia, in order to fulfill the word of the Lord spoken by Jeremiah, the Lord moved the heart of Cyrus king of Persia to make a proclamation throughout his realm and also to put it in writing: 'This is what Cyrus king of Persia says: "The Lord, the God of heaven, has given me all the kingdoms of the earth and He has appointed me to build a temple for Him at Jerusalem in Judah. Any of his people among you may go up, and may the Lord their God be with them." (2 Chronicles 36:22–23)

God will give his faithful ones and prayer warriors a burden to pray for and to act on. When He raised Lazarus from the dead, He commanded others to remove the grave clothes. "When He had said this, Jesus called in a loud voice, 'Lazarus, come out!' The dead man came out, his hands and feet wrapped with strips of linen and a cloth around his face. Jesus said to them, 'Take off the grave clothes and let Him go.'" (John 11:43–44). When we are obedient steadfast and full of faith, a heart and a city (like Jerusalem) can be restored. Jesus, our High Priest, will rebuild the walls of salvation through his shed blood on the cross. Through your prayers, trust, obedience, and perseverance, He will restore your heart as well.

Nehemiah was a cupbearer to the king of Persia, Artaxerxes. The cup-bearer brought the king's wine and certified that it was not poisoned. So He needed to be trustworthy. This could be a very influential po-sition. Cupbearers quite often became close advisors to the king. God placed the burden of repairing the walls of Jerusalem on Nehemiah's heart because of his humility, integrity, and trustworthiness just like the obedience of Jesus Christ to God. "And being found in appearance as a man, He humbled Himself by becoming obedient to death—even death on a cross! Therefore God exalted Him to the highest place and gave Him the name that is above every name, that in the name of Jesus, every knee should bow, in heaven and on earth and under the earth, and every tongue acknowledge that Jesus Christ is Lord, to the glory of God the Father" (Philippians 2:8–11).

The name of Jesus in itself means to save. It is from the Hebrew term Yehoshua/Jehoshua, contracted to Joshua, which means "Yahweh saves" (or "Yahweh is salvation").

Israel's sins that led to their captivity and the issues of your heart are both consequences of sin. The Israelites were not faithful in heart. The pain in your heart may be from the consequences of someone else's sin or yours or both. Bad choices were made, and you got hurt in the process.

The Israelites suffered many years while in captivity, oppressed by the Babylonians and Assyrians. The northern kingdom of Israel was taken into captivity by the Assyrians around 732–722 BC, and the southern kingdom of Judah went into captivity to the Babylonians in three deportations between 597 and 586 BC. God warned them over and over through prophets, but their hearts were not faithful to God. In crossing over into the Promised Land, the Lord had given them the command to destroy all their enemies, but they did not. They left some of the Canaanites, and the book of Judges deals with the effects of their disobedience. Like society today, if you allow a little bit of worldly values in here and a little there before long, you will be desensitized, and you slowly drift away from God. This is what happened to the Israelites. They would drift away from God and into the sin of worshiping the false gods and idols of the land. In their sin and disobedience, the Lord would discipline them. They would cry out to God, and He would send a judge to lead them back to Him and deliver them. This continued over and over; their hearts were not devoted to God.

When you give into the carnal desires of the world such as partying, gambling, being unfaithful, and having sex before marriage, you are doing the same thing the Israelites did. And in all the issues listed above, sooner or later, destruction follows, and heartache happens. God says in 1 Peter 1:16, "Be holy because I am holy."

This is impossible to do on our own, but with the Holy Spirit within us, we are able. It is the love of God shining through us and our devotion to Him that gives us strength and the desire to obey Him. We have the strength of the Holy Spirit to overcome any obstacle and resist all the enemy's temptations as long as we stay close to God. What you put in is what you will get out. No food, your body gets sick; no spiritual food, your spirit gets sick; but with the Spirit, you are strong. "For I can do everything through Christ, who gives me strength." (Philippians 4:13). In his strength, we can stand firm.

In Daniel 1:6–7, Daniel and his friends were taken into the king's service and were given pagan names of false gods. Daniel, whose name means "God is Judge," was given Belteshazzar, which means "May Bel protect his life." Hananiah, whose name means "Yahweh is gracious," was given Shadrach, which means "Command of Aku" (the moon god). Mishael, whose name means "who is what God is?" which means "who compares to God?" was given Meshach, which means "who is what Aku is?" Lastly, Azariah, which means "whom Yahweh helps," was given Abednego, which means "servant of Nebo," the fire god.

"Then the king ordered Ashpenaz, chief of his court officials, to bring into the king's service some of the Israelites from the royal family and the nobility— young men without any physical defect, handsome, showing aptitude for every kind of learning, well informed, quick to understand, and qualified to serve in the king's palace. He was to teach them the language and literature of the Babylonians. The king assigned them a daily amount of food and wine from the king's table. They were to be trained for three years, and after that, they were to enter the king's service. Among those who were chosen were some from Judah: Daniel, Hananiah, Mishael, and Azariah.

The chief official gave them new names: to Daniel, the name Belteshazzar; to Hananiah, Shadrach; to Mishael, Meshach; and to Azariah, Abednego. But Daniel resolved not to defile Himself with the royal food and wine, and He asked the chief official for permission not to defile Himself this way." (Daniel 1:3–8)

In each instance, they were given pagan names opposite to the meaning of their true name to corrupt their principles and morals. Sound familiar? They were trying to turn them into "one of them" and change their character, worship their gods and wild living, which was what was meant by the "moon god," the "nightlife."

We know this by verse 8 in which they tried to make them eat the royal foods. Society's norm is to live the nightlife, club, and bar hopping, and if you don't, there is something wrong with you. "What good is it for someone to gain the whole world, yet forfeit their soul?" (Mark 8:36).

How often do we experience the same thing from friends, relatives, coworkers, and schools trying to change us and our children from the person we have become through Jesus Christ to be more like them and the "ways of the world." "Do not love the world or anything in the world. If anyone loves the world, love for the Father is not in them. For everything in the world—the lust of the flesh, the lust of the eyes, and the pride of life—comes not from the Father but from the world. The world and its desires pass away, but whoever does the will of God lives forever." (1 John 2:15–17)

Living a holy life through Jesus is possible through his strength. The fun doesn't stop; you just stop paying the price for temporary pleasures and receive the blessed and highly favored life and permanent peace of being a child of God. Daniel and his friends took a stand for their faith and decided the love of God was more important, and God miraculously brought them through everything the enemy threw their way. Daniel was thrown into the lion's den, and Shadrach, Meshach, and Abednego— who were Hananiah, Mishael, and Azariah—were thrown into a fiery furnace. Each one was not harmed, not burned, and Jesus was in the fire with them. What a testimony!

The heartache you are suffering is from the oppression of the enemy due to the wrong inflicted on you. Long periods of dealing with oppression and heartache will cause wrong mindsets. These wrong mindsets will cause insecurity, despair, low self-esteem, depression, hopelessness, and pride to settle into your heart—similar to a garden of weeds. Overgrown within your heart, they block any room for the fruit of the Spirit to grow. Has your peace disappeared? Have you become impatient, or edgy? And the kindness and goodness, forgiving nature you once had when you were first saved became something from your distant past? Then you have weeds that need to be pulled. Have you become stagnant in your spiritual walk from the rubble in your heart caused by all the pain? God wants to uproot those plants but will not take what you will not give up.

"Every plant that My heavenly Father has not planted will be pulled up by the roots." (Matthew. 15:13)

Nehemiah's deep desire to repair the broken wall of Jerusalem was placed there by God. We know this because He was in service to the king. He served Him daily, and yet the king allowed Nehemiah to go to Jerusalem to repair the wall knowing this would not be a quick venture. The king also made it possible for timber to be provided. "And may I have a letter to Asaph, keeper of the royal park, so He will give me timber to make beams for the gates of the citadel by the temple and for the city wall and for the residence I will occupy? And because the gracious hand of my God was on me, the king granted my requests." (Nehemiah 2:8)

Even the meaning of the name of Nehemiah shows that God was reaching out to his people to restore them. His name means "Yahweh consoles." He went to inspect the wall to see what He was up against and learn how to proceed.

"By night I went out through the Valley Gate toward the Jackal Well and the Dung Gate, examining the walls of Jerusalem, which had been broken down, and its gates, which had been destroyed by fire. Then I moved on toward the Fountain Gate and the King's Pool, but there was not enough room for my mount to get through; so I went up the valley by night, examining the wall. Finally, I turned back and reentered through the Valley Gate. The officials did not know where I had gone or what I was doing, because as yet I had said nothing to the Jews or the priests or nobles or officials or any others who would be doing the work." (Nehemiah 2:13–16)

You need to do the same. You need to examine your heart and allow God to show you just how deeply hurt you really are and how important it is for you to allow God to heal your heart. I did not realize just how broken my heart was until I began to seek God's healing and allow Him to show me.

"Praise the Lord, my soul; all my inmost being, praise His holy name. Praise the Lord, my soul, and forget not all His benefits—who forgives all your sins and heals all your diseases, who redeems your life from the pit and crowns you with love and compassion, who satisfies your desires with good things so that your youth is renewed like the eagles." (Psalms 103:1–5)

Nehemiah could not get through the Fountain Gate, which is a symbol for the Holy Spirit, and the King's Pool which is a symbol for the fruit of the Spirit. "Whoever believes in me, as Scripture has said, rivers of living water will flow from within them" (John 7:38). It was due to the rubble of the torn-down wall. The Holy Spirit cannot get through your heart as well due to the rubble of emotions caused by all the pain. Nehemiah had to enter through the Valley Gate, which stands for humility. Before you can go any further, you need to admit you have a problem.

Pride keeps saying, "There is nothing wrong with me," when your actions and the overflow of your mouth prove otherwise, not to mention the lack of spiritual growth. "God opposes the proud but gives grace to the humble" (James 4:6). God will confront and show you areas of your heart that are filled with sin or heartache so He can lead you to forgiveness, healing, and restoration. He confronted Adam and Eve in the garden when they disobeyed to bring their sin out in the open, and their sweet fellowship could be restored as it was before. Sin left unrepented of and heartache held inside is an open door and a tool for Satan to use against you and hurt you even more. "Adam and his wife were both naked, and they felt no shame" (Genesis 2:25). This verse means that there was nothing hidden in their hearts—no sin—and they felt no shame, only peace. You need to humble yourself and admit that you do have a deeply wounded heart in need of repair. When you rid yourself of the root of pride by humbling yourself and surrendering all to God, it allows you to proceed through to the road of recovery.

With all the rubble in front of the Fountain Gate and Kings Pool, Nehemiah could not enter, and all the pain in your heart has created a wall of rubble from the ruins and the residue of the past that has overwhelmed your heart. The fruit of the Spirit, which is God's peace and joy, etc., cannot get through. "But the Fruit of the Spirit is love, joy, peace, patience, kindness, goodness, faithfulness, gentleness, and self-control. Against such things, there is no law" (Galatians 5:22–23).

Pool in this text is from the Hebrew origin Barak—pool meaning "reservoir," and Barak meaning "abundantly blessed."

"Praise be to the God and Father of our Lord Jesus Christ, who has blessed us in the heavenly realms with every spiritual blessing in Christ." (Ephesians 1:3)

God has a reservoir of abundant blessings stored up for you, but you must allow Him to cleanse your heart. To do this, you must admit that you need his help and invite Him into every area that needs to be healed. Next, due to the pain in your heart, I am sure, just like me, it caused you to react and speak in ways that are not Christ-like. So you need to repent of any sins. This takes us through to the next gate, which is the Dung Gate and it represents a place of cleansing. As you draw close to God through prayer and confession, He will draw close to you and begin the healing process.

"Submit yourselves, then, to God. Resist the devil, and He will flee from you. Come near to God and He will come near to you. Wash your hands, you sinners, and purify your hearts, you double-minded. Grieve, mourn, and wail. Change your laughter to mourning and your joy to gloom. Humble yourselves before the Lord, and He will lift you up." (James 4:7–10)

The Israelites felt disgraced at seeing the walls torn down. The walls of Jerusalem were a symbol of strength and a right relationship with God. This troubled Nehemiah as he saw this. "Then I said to them, 'You see the trouble we are in: Jerusalem lies in ruins, and its gates have been burned with fire. Come, let us rebuild the wall of Jerusalem, and we will no longer be in disgrace." (Nehemiah 2:17)

God is just as heartbroken to know the walls of your heart are broken and are no longer fortified with his strength. Sin and heartache brought on by others left in your heart to fester and take root instead of giving over to God will tear down the protective walls of God. God longs to repair those walls and restore your broken heart, healing you completely. "Yet the Lord longs to be gracious to you; therefore He will rise up to show you compassion. For the Lord is a God of justice. Blessed are all who wait for Him!" (Isaiah 30:18)

The Lord sent Nehemiah to rebuild the walls. "The Lord builds up Jerusalem; He gathers the exiles of Israel. He heals the brokenhearted and binds up their wounds" (Psalms 147:2–3). He will, if not already, send people into your life as well to be his extended hands, feet, voice, and heart to repair the walls of your heart. In your brokenness, dare to trust God. Allow Him to take you back in time to each painful event, each time someone broke your heart, and each painful memory and walk you through to forgiveness so you can let go once and for all. Doing it God's way will remove all the heartache and pain completely and leave in its place the healing waters of his joy and love. "Fill my heart with joy when their grain and new wine abound." (Psalms 4:7) Ask Him, and He will come to your rescue. "You do not have because you do not ask God." (James 4:2)

God longs to heal your heart. Let Him in so He can.

"When the Lord brought back the captives to Zion, we were like men who dreamed. Our mouths were filled with laughter, our tongues with songs of joy. Then it was said among the nations, "The Lord has done great things for them." The Lord has done great things for us, and we are filled with joy. Restore our fortunes, O Lord, like streams in the Negev. Those who sow in tears will reap with songs of joy. He who goes out weeping, carrying seed to sow, will return with songs of joy, carrying sheaves with Him." (Psalm 126)

2

~

Discover The Cracks

I used to be a bookkeeper for a concrete construction company. They mainly installed new foundations for commercial projects. However, at times, they did do residential and even the repair of existing foundations. To repair an existing one with cracks, the first step is to discover where the cracks began.

Concerning our hearts, in order to obtain complete healing, you need to do the same. You need to go back to the beginning, to the very first onset of pain you experienced. Otherwise, if any painful event or memory is left and not given to God, you will not be totally healed. There will still be heartache and a heaviness in your heart left behind to keep you down like an infection in your heart.

There is a surgical procedure called debridement (pronounced debridement), which is the removal of dead or damaged tissue to improve the healing potential of the remaining. If it is not done right and damaged tissue is left behind, an infection will set in (from Wikipedia), which is what will happen to your heart if you do not surrender all to God. It will eventually surface and more than likely in a way damaging to your emotions, health, and even your existing relationships.

When people and events hurt us over and over, it is similar to a cracked foundation. Our hearts get broken and leave cracks that weaken us. It leaves room for the enemy to get in and with several enemy spirits such as bitterness, resentment, lack of forgiveness, anger, self-pity, depression, despair, and hopelessness. If not dealt with and given over to God, the maker of your heart—to replace with his healing joy, peace, and love—they will take root creating a stronghold. A stronghold is a fortress, and in relation to your spirit, it is a demonic fortress that only the power of God can uproot. Left in your heart without seeking the help and love of God, it can destroy your life. Many people who are severely overwhelmed with depression become suicidal.

"When an impure spirit comes out of a person, it goes through arid places seeking rest and does not find it. Then it says, 'I will return to the house I left.' When it arrives, it finds the house swept clean and put in order. Then it goes and takes seven other spirits more wicked than itself, and they go in and live there. And the final condition of that person is worse than the first." (Luke 11:24–26)

A broken heart weakens your defense system, and you become too weary from the oppression to fight off Satan's attacks. But God—He will not let you stay that way! He will, if not already, send people into your life to lead you through or initiate the process of your healing. "He refreshes my soul. He guides me along the right paths for His name's sake." (Psalms 23:3)

When God wanted to repair the temple, He moved in the heart of King Cyrus of Persia, a Gentile. He can use anyone, anywhere. God moved King Cyrus's heart to send people to repair the temple. "In the first year of Cyrus king of Persia, in order to fulfill the word of the Lord spoken by Jeremiah, the Lord moved the heart of Cyrus king of Persia to make a proclamation throughout his realm and also to put it in writing: 'This is what Cyrus king of Persia says: "The Lord, the God of heaven, has given me all the kingdoms of the earth and He has appointed me to build a temple for Him at Jerusalem in Judah. Any of His people among you may go up, and may the Lord their God be with them." (2 Chronicles 36:22–23)

King Cyrus even provided materials for rebuilding and filling the temple. That is my God! "Any of His people among you may go up to Jerusalem in Judah and build the temple of the Lord, the God of Israel, the God who is in Jerusalem, and may their God be with them. And in any locality where survivors may now be living, the people are to provide them with silver and gold, with goods and livestock, and with freewill offerings for the temple of God in Jerusalem." (Ezra 1:3–4)

When God says, "Enough is enough," and wants to heal and deliver you, He will provide what is needed and who is needed to do it. To begin the healing process, you must, as said earlier, go back to the beginning to discover where the first crack, the first onset of pain began. Every bit of rubble needs to be cleared out for complete healing and for the fruit of the Holy Spirit to have clear passage. Sometimes Jesus healed instantly, and at other times, it was in stages. In one case, He made mud and put it on the man's eyes. "After saying this, He spit on the ground, made some mud with the saliva, and put it on the man's eyes. 'Go,' He told Him, 'wash in the Pool of Siloam' (this word means 'sent'). So the man went and washed, and came home seeing" (John 9:6–7). We are created from the dust of the earth. "Then the Lord God formed a man from the dust of the ground and breathed into his nostrils the breath of life and the man became a living being."(Genesis 2:7)

Jesus used that which was from the beginning to heal his eyes. This is why sometimes with pain that goes deep within our hearts, it may take a while—a process starting at the beginning and giving it over to God and allowing Him to help you to forgive and let go, giving it all over to Him to deal with so it will not control you any longer. "'I have the right to do anything,' you say—but not everything is beneficial. 'I have the right to do anything'—but I will not be mastered by anything." (1 Corinthians 6:12) Jesus died to set us free and not be mastered by anything. Satan is the one who tries to enslave you and keep you in bondage to your emotional pain and addictions that you may turn to for temporary peace. Why settle for temporary when you can have permanent peace through God? "They promise them freedom, while they themselves are slaves of depravity—for "people are slaves to whatever has mastered them." (2 Peter 2:19)

God wants to heal and bless you; Satan wants to destroy you. "The thief comes only to steal and kill and destroy; I have come that they may have life and have it to the full" (John 10:10). Satan does not want you to seek God. He does not want you to go to Him in prayer for help, and he will bombard you with thoughts of doubt and hopelessness such as, "Even God cannot help you," "God has forgotten you," and "I have done too much for God to love or help me." That is a lie! Satan is a liar! God says, "I will never leave you nor forsake you."

"He was a murderer from the beginning, not holding to the truth, for there is no truth in Him. When he lies, he speaks his native language, for he is a liar and the father of lies" (John 8:44). God is the creator of your heart, and He sent Jesus to die for your sins and the sins of the world to give you eternal salvation. He wants to save your life and not destroy it. "For God so loved the world that He gave his one and only Son, that whoever believes in Him shall not perish but have eternal life" (John 3:16). Every good gift is from above. "Every good and perfect gift is from above, coming down from the Father of the heavenly lights, who does not change like shifting shadows." (James 1:17)

Trust your heart to the one who created it and breathed life into it. He wants to give you hope and not take it away. "'For I know the plans I have for you,' declares the Lord, 'plans to prosper you and not to harm you, plans to give you hope and a future. Then you will call on me and come and pray to me, and I will listen to you. You will seek me and find me when you seek me with all your heart. I will be found by you,' declares the Lord, 'and will bring you back from captivity." (Jeremiah 29:11–14) When thoughts of despair and hopelessness, fear and worry, etc. come into your mind, trash them. You do not have to take ownership of them and dwell on them. "We demolish arguments and every pretension that sets itself up against the knowledge of God, and we take captive every thought to make it obedient to Christ." (2 Corinthians 10:5) Instead of dwelling on the thoughts that bring you down, replace them with promises of God found in the Word.

"Rejoice in the Lord always. I will say it again: Rejoice! Let your gentleness be evident to all. The Lord is near. Do not be anxious about anything, but in every situation, by prayer and petition, with thanksgiving, present your requests to God. And the peace of God, which transcends all understanding, will guard your hearts and your minds in Christ Jesus. Finally, brothers and sisters, whatever is true, whatever is noble, whatever is right, whatever is pure, whatever is lovely, whatever is admirable—if anything is excellent or praiseworthy—think about such things. Whatever you have learned or received or heard from me, or seen in me—put it into practice. And the God of peace will be with you." (Philippians 4:4–9)

The heaviness your heart feels is due to all the baggage of bad emotions you have allowed to stay and settle in your heart. Yes, I said allow—you have a choice! You do not have to stay angry and depressed. God wants to help. He wants to heal you and uproot all that is not from Him, but He will not force Himself on you. Ask and He will be there to help. "Every plant that my heavenly Father has not planted will be pulled up by the roots." (Matthew. 15:13)

Nehemiah had to inspect the wall before rebuilding it. Salvation in itself is the great exchange of God's eternal love and salvation for our faith and devotion, but God, as our Heavenly Father has to set it firm in our heart to persevere no matter how difficult things get and what or who come up against us. Spiritual growth much like natural is not always easy, but to grow and continue the path to your destiny you must persevere. The Lord had to set that same perseverance in Nehemiah's heart until the job of repairing the wall was done. He knew God was directing Him and God would protect Him and his workers.

As you allow God to travel through the process with you, He will guard your heart, and the Holy Spirit will give you reminders to keep you on the right path. "After I looked things over, I stood up and said to the nobles, the officials, and the rest of the people, "Don't be afraid of them. Remember the Lord, who is great and awesome, and fight for your families, your sons and your daughters, your wives, and your homes." (Nehemiah 4:14)

The process of repairing your heart must start not only at the first incident that broke it but also in being a child of God most importantly. My dad was not responsible for the emotional and physical well-being of any other children other than his, and if God is not your Father, then it is the same with Him—he is not responsible. So if you are not, then that is easy to change.

Just pray this prayer sincerely from your heart.
Dear Heavenly Father,
I believe in you and in Jesus, you're Son. I believe He died for me and for my sins on the cross to forgive my sins. I ask in His name for you to forgive me of my sins (name your sins as you pray) and cleanse my heart of all unrighteousness. I also ask for you to help me to forgive others in return for your strength and your love. I ask for the Holy Spirit of Jesus Christ to come in and live and dwell within my heart and also to baptize me in the Holy Spirit. I now accept that I am now saved and born again and am your child, a child of God!
I ask this in Jesus's name. Amen.

If you just sincerely prayed that prayer and meant it, then welcome to the family of God, and congratulations because you are now officially on the road to recovery—to the restoration and healing of your heart!

When Nehemiah and the people started the work of repairing the wall, they had to start at the beginning, which was the Sheep Gate and symbolized Jesus, our Lord, and Shepherd. "I am the Good Shepherd. The Good Shepherd lays down His life for the sheep." (John 10:11) This is represented by Eliashib the high priest, who took over rebuilding the wall by this section. He rebuilt the wall as far as the tower of Hananel, which is from the Hebrew words chanan and el meaning "God is gracious." In his mercy and grace, He initiated the repair of the temple through King Cyrus and Ezra and the wall through Nehemiah. God is the "Repairer of broken walls." He initiated the redemption of mankind by sending his own Son and our High Priest to take our place on the cross.

"The Lord looked and was displeased that there was no justice. He saw that there was no one, and He was appalled that there was no one to intervene; so His own arm achieved salvation for Him, and His own righteousness sustained Him. He put on righteousness as his breastplate, and the helmet of salvation on his head; He put on the garments of vengeance and wrapped Himself in zeal as in a cloak." (Isaiah 59:15-17)

The next part of the wall was the Fish Gate, which was near the market meaning provision and discipleship. God provided salvation, and God will also provide all your needs. "And my God will meet all your needs according to the riches of his glory in Christ Jesus" (Philippians 4:19). He would also supply through his people and the Gentiles what was needed for the repair. Trust God to help you with everything needed to repair your heart as well.

It was not easy repairing the wall. Satan does not want God's children whole and full of joy because when we are, our life becomes a testimony and more people are saved, encouraged, healed, and blessed because of it.

Satan wants you down, depressed, and suicidal. He wants to destroy you! "Be alert and of sober mind. Your enemy the devil prowls around like a roaring lion looking for someone to devour." (1 Peter 5:8)

When Nehemiah began, Sanballat did not like it. Like Sanballat, he represents Satan, and he sets out to stop the repair. Sanballat kept trying to interfere by using fear and intimidation tactics. That is what Satan will try to do to you as you begin. He will cause things to happen and use people to hurt you and bring you down. Beware ahead of time, and just know that he is a creature of habit, and prepare yourself ahead of time. Be read up on the Word and its promises; it is living and active and gives you strength when you need it. You must be determined and stand firm. "If you do not stand firm in your faith, you will not stand at all." (Isaiah 7:9)

In rebuilding the wall, the people kept a sword in their hands. Some worked, and some stood guard. "When our enemies heard that we were aware of their plot and that God had frustrated it, we all returned to the wall, each to our own work. From that day on, half of my men did the work, while the other half were equipped with spears, shields, bows, and armor. The officers posted themselves behind all the people of Judah." (Nehemiah 4:15–16)

Their weapons symbolize the Bible. "But we prayed to our God and posted a guard day and night to meet this threat." (Nehemiah 4:9) "The Bible is our weapon! "May the praise of God be in their mouths and a double-edged sword in their hands, to inflict vengeance on the nations and punishment on the peoples, to bind their kings with fetters, their nobles with shackles of iron, to carry out the sentence written against them—this is the glory of all His faithful people." (Psalms 149:6–9)

God in all His power spoke the Word; his power is behind it! All it takes is faith in your heart to believe it and your mouth to speak it! "The Spirit gives life; the flesh counts for nothing. The words I have spoken to you—they are full of the Spirit and life." (John 6:63)

Even Jesus used the Word when He was being tempted in the desert. The Bible is your weapon against Satan. Read it and speak it, and it will come alive in your heart, and the Spirit of the Lord will activate it and manifest it! "For the Word of God is alive and active. Sharper than any double-edged sword, it penetrates even to dividing soul and spirit, joints and marrow; it judges the thoughts and attitudes of the heart." (Hebrews 4:12)

God exalts His Word. "I will bow down toward your holy temple and will praise your Name for your unfailing love and your faithfulness, for you have exalted above all things your Name and your Word." (Psalms 138:2) The Word of God is the best thing you have to pray. It is alive, and it will not return void; the word is our food and our weapon. When God speaks through his own Spirit directly, written or by his Spirit through your voice and heart, it will accomplish its purpose, and the Word will be fulfilled!

"As the heavens are higher than the earth, so are My ways higher than your ways and My thoughts than your thoughts. As the rain and the snow come down from heaven, and do not return to it without watering the earth and making it bud and flourish, so that it yields seed for the sower and bread for the eater, so is My Word that goes out from My mouth: It will not return to Me empty, but will accomplish what I desire and achieve the purpose for which I sent it." (Isaiah 55:9–11)

The Bible is food for your soul just as physical food is to the body. They both give strength: one to the body, and one to the spirit. If you find yourself weak and weary and not able to stand against the enemies' attacks, then examine your daily routine. Do you make time for God and for reading the Bible? If not, then that is your problem! Your spirit is not getting fed!

Then Jesus declared, "I am the bread of life. Whoever comes to me will never go hungry, and whoever believes in me will never be thirsty. But as I told you, you have seen me and still you do not believe. All those the Father gives me will come to me, and whoever comes to me I will never drive away. For I have come down from heaven not to do my will but to do the will of Him who sent me. And this is the will of Him who sent me that I shall lose none of all those He has given me, but raise them up at the last day. For my Father's will is that everyone who looks to the Son and believes in Him shall have eternal life, and I will raise them up at the last day." (John 6:35–40)

When weeds are pulled from a garden, they get lighter when all the dirt is shaken off. When you give your pain to God, He will use other people and trials to do the shaking for Him—your heart will get lighter. When you spend time with God, you will draw close to Him and will discover that it is because of his great love for you that He allows certain events to take place. They are to teach you and draw that which is not from Him out. "Consider it pure joy, my brothers and sisters, whenever you face trials of many kinds because you know that the testing of your faith produces perseverance. Let perseverance finish its work so that you may be mature and complete, not lacking anything." (James 1:2–4)

When you choose to see this through to completion and go through each painful memory, letting go and forgiving all involved, your heart will feel lighter than air—just like weeds when all the dirt falls off. Allow God to shake you a little. Persevere through to the end. "Blessed is the one who perseveres under trial because, having stood the test, that person will receive the crown of life that the Lord has promised to those who love Him." (James 1:12)

God will take care of those who hurt you. He will not leave the guilty unpunished, but He will do it in a way that will penetrate their hearts. "The Lord is slow to anger but great in power; the Lord will not leave the guilty unpunished. His way is in the whirlwind and the storm, and clouds are the dust of His feet" (Nahum 1:3). So give Him your pain and allow Him to take care of those that hurt you in his way. In the end, they too might end up saved and wanting to make things right with you. "This is good and pleases God our Savior, who wants all people to be saved and to come to a knowledge of the truth" (1 Timothy 2:4). God wants those who hurt you to know and admit and repent as well. If his wrath is needed to bring that about then, his wrath will be shown.

"Do not repay anyone evil for evil. Be careful to do what is right in the eyes of everyone. If it is possible, as far as it depends on you, live at peace with everyone. Do not take revenge, my dear friends, but leave room for God's wrath, for it is written: "It is mine to avenge; I will repay," says the Lord. On the contrary: "If your enemy is hungry, feed Him; if He is thirsty, give Him something to drink. In doing this, you will hear burning coals on his head." Do not be overcome by evil, but overcome evil with good." (Romans 12:17–21)

When you give it all over to God, then all that is left is for you to concentrate on being emotionally and spiritually healed. Repent of your own inability to forgive, and let go and move on. "Therefore I tell you, whatever you ask for in prayer, believe that you have received it, and it will be yours. And when you stand praying, if you hold anything against anyone, forgive them, so that your Father in heaven may forgive you your sins." (Mark 11:24–26)

The purpose of revisiting each event and each person who hurt you is to give them over to God and let go and forgive them. In giving anything to anyone, it is not theirs until you give it. The heartache, that thing that hurt you so deeply, is not God's until you give it to Him. Releasing it to Him and forgiving will accomplish this. If you do not, then it will remain planted in your heart and will continue to cause you grief, pain, and anger.

God told the Israelites to move on from Mt. Horeb (or Mt. Sinai), and He is telling you to do the same. "The Lord, our God, said to us at Horeb, 'You have stayed long enough at this mountain." (Deuteronomy 1:6) Horeb is from the Hebrew chareb or choreb meaning "Waste, bitterness, the inability to forgive, depression, hopeless, etc. are all wastes that clutter your heart—leaving no room for the fruit of the Spirit to grow and flourish, giving you the fullness of the joy of the Lord.

It is a waste of precious time that you could be experiencing God's peace and joy and fullness of life. What was an eleven-day journey that took them forty years! What a waste! At this time, they had been traveling for thirty-eight years and God said enough! Move on! Their lack of faith and obedience kept them there longer than God had wished. But their stubborn hearts prolonged the journey. It did not have to be that way. "The Israelites are stubborn, like a stubborn heifer. How then can the Lord pasture them like lambs in a meadow?" (Hosea 4:16)

Do not let stubbornness, self-will, pride, and rebellion keep you from your joy and your destiny in Christ! "Does the Lord delight in burnt offerings and sacrifices as much as in obeying the Lord? To obey is better than sacrifice, and to heed is better than the fat of rams. For rebellion is like the sin of divination and arrogance like the evil of idolatry." (1 Samuel 15:22–23)

Allow the Lord to help you discover each crack in your heart, step by step and one by one.

Step-by-Step
Step-by-step, you lead me. Step-by-step, I follow. You lead me in the everlasting way.
Though darkness may surround me, the light of your glory illuminates my path.
Darkness is not dark to you, so in childlike faith, I follow.

Though darkness may surround, darkness is not dark to you. The light of your glory lights my way.

So step-by-step, I follow.

You lead me in the way everlasting.

Step-by-step, you lead me. Step-by-step, I follow. You lead me in the everlasting way.

You bore my sins, you wore my pain—in it, I am healed.

By the cross, you carried all my sins, all my pain, and all my worries are nailed to it. So step-by-step, I follow.

You rose to glory and left life, liberty, and purity behind through your Holy Spirit. So step-by-step, I follow.

Step-by-step, you lead me. Step-by-step, I follow. You lead me in the everlasting way until finally, those steps lead me home.

God will remove the pain and replace it with his healing love and joy as you hand it over, letting Him lead step-by-step doing it his way.

"Restore to me the joy of Your salvation and grant me a willing spirit, to sustain me." (Psalms 51:12)

PART 2: Raise Up The Age-Old Foundation

"And will raise up the age-old foundations."

3

～

Discover The Cause

In the last chapter, we discussed discovering the cracks, going back to the beginning, and discovering where the pain began along with remembering each event or person who hurt you. Part II of this book deals with raising up the age-old foundation and concerning healing your heart, you are essentially taking your heart back to when you were first saved. Remember how you felt? Remember the overwhelming joy that filled your heart? God wants to fill it with that same joy once again! "Then my soul will rejoice in the Lord and delight in His salvation." (Psalms 35:9)

In this chapter, in order to get back the joy of your salvation now that you discovered where it all began, you need to discover the cause. Discover how and what happened in order to learn from it and allow God to dispel the lies and replace them with the truth and provide for you what was missing or taken from you. Some events might have been purely at the hand of someone else, and others were a combination of what they did or said and your reaction. This needs to be identified so you can repent of any sin on your part and learn from it and the forgiveness given. Then you can move on and know how to handle the situation correctly if the same type of thing happens again. Satan is a creature of habit, and He knows your weaknesses and will try to use them again, but this time, you will be prepared. Clearing up the past will also keep you from having one for Satan to bring up in the future to use against you.

In repairing a concrete foundation once they find where the cracks begin and identify what caused it, they can repair the damage. You cannot cover up the damage to your heart; it needs to be repaired. Covering up will only cause it to surface again and again until you deal with it. Forgiving those who have hurt you and seeking forgiveness from those you have wronged is all a part of the process of clearing out the waste or the rubble in your heart so the fruit of the Spirit can grow once again.

Emotions such as depression, pride, bitterness, the inability to forgive, doubt, worry, fear, anger, resentment, etc. are like a huge boulder that covers a well and keeps you from the water within. In our main verse, Jesus is the Repairer of broken walls, but He will not go beyond your own will. The word foundation, as used in our verse, is from the Hebrew yasad or mowcad meaning "absolute, construct." Foundations need to be strong and without cracks that weaken it, in order to hold tall buildings, columns, and houses on it. There is only one foundation that will perfect our hearts and only one that will heal it perfectly.

"Why do you call me, 'Lord, Lord, 'and do not do what I say? As for every-one who comes to me and hears my words and puts them into practice, I will show you what they are like. They are like a man building a house, who dug down deep and laid the foundation on rock. When a flood came, the torrent struck that house but could not shake it, because it was well-built. But the one who hears my words and does not put them into practice is like a man who built a house on the ground without a foundation. The moment the torrent struck that house, it collapsed and its destruction was complete." (Luke 6:46–49)

When our hearts are built on a firm foundation, Jesus, we can get through anything! "In this way, they will lay up treasure for themselves as a firm foundation for the coming age, so that they may take hold of the life that is truly life." (1 Timothy 6:19)

Part of ensuring a strong foundation is to use the right concrete mix for the right project. Concrete mix designs range from 3,000 to 7,000 psi. Psi stands for pounds of pressure per square inch. The soil and the conditions of the area determine what level of psi mix design you use along with the type of project such as a house, commercial building, bridge, or even driveway. A good engineer and contractor will know which one to use for each project. God, the Creator of our hearts, knows exactly what is in our hearts and what it will take to cleanse and heal it. "If we had forgotten the name of our God or spread out our hands to a foreign god, would not God have discovered it since He knows the secrets of the heart?" (Psalms 44:20–21)

Knowing God and trusting that He knows your heart and knowing who He is, what He has done for you, what He wants to do for you, and what He can do for you and will do for you is an important part of the process of obtaining complete healing. It will help you to be as patient with Him in the process as He has been with you throughout your life. This leads us to the next part of the wall they repaired in Nehemiah, the Jeshanah or Old Gate. The Hebrew meaning is "withered, shabby, or lifeless, as in sleep."

"This is why it is said: 'Wake up, sleeper, rise from the dead, and Christ will shine on you." (Ephesians 5:14) This gate represents the "Old man, old self." It represents your old lifestyle—the way in which you used to live and God is not just repairing old man, He is creating a new man through Jesus Christ. Your old ways kept you in sin when you received Jesus. You are a new creation in Christ and purified from sin. "Therefore, if anyone is in Christ, He is a new creation." (2 Corinthians 5:17) You have his Holy Spirit within you, but your mind is still the same. It is your heart that has changed. Your mind needs to be renewed day by day.

"You were taught, with regard to your former way of life, to put off your old self, which is being corrupted by its deceitful desires; to be made new in the attitude of your minds; and to put on the new self, created to be like God in true righteousness and holiness." (Ephesians 4:22–24)

When we surrender all to Christ and allow Him to cleanse every part of our soul—which is our mind, will, and emotions—we will be renewed. The way in which we can let Him renew our minds is through reading the Word of God daily. "Therefore, I urge you, brothers and sisters, in view of God's mercy, to offer your bodies as a living sacrifice, holy and pleasing to God—this is your true and proper worship. Do not conform to the pattern of this world, but be transformed by the renewing of your mind. Then you will be able to test and approve what God's will is—His good, pleasing, and perfect will." (Romans 12:1–2)

Your flesh will always want to please self, which will always get in the way of your victory. Living only to please yourself will eventually hurt others and this is probably how you were hurt by someone else following after their flesh. We are called to consider others better than ourselves, and the love of Jesus is all about loving others, humbling yourself, and sacrificing your needs for the sake of others.

The love of Jesus does not exalt self; it exalts others. "Do nothing out of selfish ambition or vain conceit, but in humility consider others better than yourselves." (Philippians 2:3)

God will use our daily life and the trials that come our way to purify us and to help us to grow spiritually and weed out the impurities and die to self. "Consider it pure joy, my brothers, whenever you face trials of many kinds because you know that the testing of your faith develops perseverance. Perseverance must finish its work so that you may be mature and complete, not lacking anything." (James 1:2–4)

To be mature in your faith, you have been purified or have undergone the baptism of fire. "I baptize you with water for repentance. But after me will come one who is more powerful than I, whose sandals I am not fit to carry. He will baptize you with the Holy Spirit and with fire." (Matthew. 3:11)

God likens the process of purification to the purifying process of gold. When gold is purified, it goes through the fire until the goldsmith can see his image in it.

"Praise be to the God and Father of our Lord Jesus Christ! In His great mercy, He has given us new birth into a living hope through the resurrection of Jesus Christ from the dead, and into an inheritance that can never perish, spoil, or fade—kept in heaven for you, who through faith are shielded by God's power until the coming of the salvation that is ready to be revealed in the last time. In this, you greatly rejoice, though now for a little while you may have had to suffer grief in all kinds of trials. These have come so that your faith—of greater worth than gold, which perishes even though refined by fire—may be proved genuine and may result in praise, glory, and honor when Jesus Christ is revealed." (1 Peter 1:3–7)

God wants to see his image in you! We should be a reflection of our Lord and Savior. This gives true glory to God. The world is affected more by your life than your words. "And we, who with unveiled faces all reflect the Lord's glory, are being transformed into his likeness with ever-increasing glory, which comes from the Lord, who is the Spirit." (2 Corinthians 3:18)

In the book of Daniel 3:20–27, Shadrach, Meshach, and Abednego are thrown into a fiery furnace, and they came forth unharmed. In fact, people saw a fourth man in the fire with them—a man who looked like a "son of the gods." This was Jesus! This passage represents the purification process of God. The Lord has years of the world to weed out of most of us when we are saved. "He replied, 'Every plant that my heavenly Father has not planted will be pulled up by the roots." (Matthew. 15:13) Yes, we are a new creation, but our minds need to be renewed.

Letting God lead you and teach you as you go through trials is dying to self—dying to the flesh. Your flesh and your mind may want to do something contrary to the Spirit, but it is your choice to obey it or God. "So I say, live by the Spirit, and you will not gratify the desires of the sinful nature. For the sinful nature desires what is contrary to the Spirit and the Spirit what is contrary to the sinful nature." (Galatians 5:16–17)

Living according to the flesh gives Satan an open door to destroy your life. "The acts of the sinful nature are obvious: sexual immorality, impurity, and debauchery; idolatry and witchcraft; hatred, discord, jealousy, fits of rage, selfish ambition, dissensions, factions, and envy; drunkenness, orgies, and the like. I warn you, as I did before, that those who live like this will not inherit the kingdom of God." (Galatians 5:19–21)

The Jeshanah or Old Gate is about God creating a new person in Christ. It is about God sanctifying us through the Holy Spirit. Through His Spirit, we are able to live a victorious life. "May God Himself, the God of peace, sanctify you through and through? May your whole spirit, soul, and body be kept blameless at the coming of our Lord Jesus Christ." (1 Thessalonians 5:23)

Living according to the Spirit will give you a life of peace, victory, love, freedom, and the fullness of life that God promises us in his Word. "The thief comes to steal, and kill and destroy; I have come that they may have life, and have it to the full." (John 10:10)

God spoke the world into existence, and He spoke it into the hearts of man, and we reap the benefits of it as his written Word. Jesus is the Word, who became flesh. "In the beginning was the Word, and the Word was with God, and the Word was God. He was with God in the beginning. Through Him all things were made; without Him, nothing was made that has been made. In Him was life, and that life was the light of all mankind. The light shines in the darkness, and the darkness has not over-come it." (John 1:1–5)

"The Word became flesh and made his dwelling among us. We have seen his glory, the glory of the one and only Son, who came from the Father, full of grace and truth" (John 1:14). You need food daily for your body to stay healthy, and the Bible daily for your communion with Him is food for your soul for your spiritual health.

The next part of the wall that was repaired was the Broad Wall, and it symbolizes our flesh, our will that stubborn will that always want its way. We are all flesh, and the flesh is weak. "Watch and pray so that you will not fall into temptation. The spirit is willing, but the flesh is weak." (Mark 14:38) The meaning of the Broad Wall is "Broad, large, liberty, wide" and is from the Hebrew root word rachab meaning "Roomy in any direction." The Old Gate was repaired to the Broad Wall, meaning death to self (to own will) in which you lived as you pleased and God has to tear down the walls of flesh in order to give you true liberty. Liberty that comes from a heart filled with God's love does not need to or want to live a life with the flesh, carnal desires, ruling over you.

"Enter through the narrow gate. For wide is the gate and broad is the road that leads to destruction, and many enter through it. But small is the gate and narrow the road that leads to life and only a few find it." (Matthew. 7:13–14) In Christ, as you mature, you die to self, to the old man, and are being made new in Christ. Living a life of sin and doing as you please will keep you bound. "For the creation was subjected to frustration, not by its own choice, but by the will of the one who subjected it, in hope that the creation itself will be liberated from its bondage to decay and brought into the glorious freedom of the children of God." (Romans 8:20–21)

Receiving Jesus as Lord of your life will set you free from the bondage of sin. Your heart is free and not bound any longer. "It is for freedom that Christ has set us free. Stand firm, then, and do not let yourselves be burdened again by a yoke of slavery." (Galatians 5:1) In Jesus, we are the righteousness of God and are totally free!

"So if the Son sets you free, you will be free indeed." (John 8:36) Sin keeps you bound with a heavy heart and restless with no peace. Jesus frees our hearts and fills us with his eternal peace and not the temporary peace the world offers.

In 2 Chronicles 25:23, Jehoash king of Israel captured Amaziah king of Judah in his own territory. God will meet you right where you are; all you have to do is call on his name, and He will save you. You do not have to clean yourself up, just call on the name of Jesus, and He will do the rest. He will tear down the walls of sin and rebuild the wall of salvation within your heart. You need to do it. You need to call on Him and ask Him in. No one can receive salvation for you. "God will give to each person according to what He has done." (Romans 2:6)

Amaziah started worshiping the gods of the people of Seir. God had to let Him know that He was not pleased, so He set Jehoash, king of Israel, against Him. King Jehoash captured Him and tore down the Broad Wall. Sometimes, in order to make room (broad, large, wide) for the fruit of the Spirit to grow, God needs to tear down some walls. He needs to tear down our walls of flesh where self-will and pride grow and only lead us into more bondage. He tears it down so the walls of Christ can be built—walls of love, peace, joy, humility, and self-control and a forgiving heart full of mercy and compassion. He needs to tear down wrong mindsets and idols—idols of self-pity, drugs, alcohol, cigarettes, etc. He needs to tear down the wall of pride, anger, lack of forgiveness, bitterness, jealousy, etc. The walls of flesh will only be a hindrance and keep us in bondage to sin. Discovering the issues you have and what caused them and then repenting and giving them over to God is part of the healing process. In this section, men and women repaired the wall.

This shows God will use both men and women to teach, disciple, preach, and bring a word or to heal. Let God transform you through the washing and renewing of your mind and heart. "But when the kindness and love of God our Savior appeared, He saves us through the washing of rebirth and renewal by the Holy Spirit, whom He poured out on us generously through Jesus Christ our Savior, so that, having been justified by his grace, we might become heirs having the hope of eternal life." (Titus 3:4–7)

"Create in me a pure heart, O God, and renew a steadfast spirit within me. Do not cast me from your presence or take your Holy Spirit from me. Restore to me the joy of your salvation and grant me a willing spirit, to sustain me." (Psalms 51:10–12)

Submit to God and allow Him to transform you and heal you so that you may go from glory to glory. He will bring you into a spacious place and liberate your heart. "They confronted me in the day of my disaster, but the Lord was my support. He brought me out into a spacious place; He rescued me because He delighted in me." (Psalms 18:18–19)

Before you were saved, most people anyway did pretty much whatever they wanted. Paul states in 1 Corinthians 6:12, "'I have the right to do anything,' you say—but not everything is beneficial. 'I have the right to do anything'— but I will not be mastered by anything." When you constantly live by what your flesh dictates, it will give you the results of it. "You, my brothers and sisters, were called to be free. But do not use your freedom to indulge the flesh; rather, serve one another humbly in love. For the entire law is fulfilled in keeping this one command: 'Love your neighbor as yourself.' If you bite and devour each other, watch out or you will be destroyed by each other." (Galatians 5:13–15)

Learning to surrender to the Lordship of Jesus Christ, you will reap the benefits and freedom of Christ. In Christ, by His Spirit, we will know what is best and what will produce fruit. True freedom is in knowing that while we are free in Christ; true liberty is not being dictated by the desires and cravings of the flesh, some of which lead to sin. "Whoever sows to please their flesh, from the flesh will reap destruction; whoever sows to please the Spirit, from the Spirit will reap eternal life. Let us not become weary in doing well, for at the proper time we will reap a harvest if we do not give up." (Galatians 6:8–9)

When we live by the guidance and direction of the Holy Spirit, we will reap the benefits of the Spirit. "Praise be to the God and Father of our Lord Jesus Christ, who has blessed us in the heavenly realms with every spiritual blessing in Christ." (Ephesians 1:3)

As you grow closer to the Lord, the desire to obey and please Him grows as well. Although there may be many choices and many directions you can take in life, if those choices lead you away from God, then they will also lead to more pain, which is what you are trying to get removed from your heart. "Enter through the narrow gate. For wide is the gate and broad is the road that leads to destruction, and many enter through it." (Matthew. 7:13)

The choice is yours and being able to have them and yet say "No" to those choices that you know will displease God is quite liberating. "This day I call the heavens and the earth as witnesses against you that I have set before your life and death, blessings and curses. Now choose life, so that you and your children may live and that you may love the Lord your God, listen to His voice, and hold fast to Him. For the Lord is your life and He will give you many years in the land He swore to give to your fathers, Abraham, Isaac, and Jacob." (Deuteronomy 30:19–20)

Learning to live by the leadership of the Holy Spirit helps you to grow spiritually and is part of the process of becoming totally healed. "Now the Lord is the Spirit, and where the Spirit of the Lord is, there is freedom." (2 Corinthians 3:17)

This leads to the next part of the wall that was repaired— the tower of ovens, meaning "furnace or overwhelming pressure." No one likes trials, but we always learn better through experience than by someone telling us what to do. "Consider it pure joy, my brothers and sisters, whenever you face trials of many kinds, because you know that the testing of your faith produces perseverance. Let perseverance finish its work so that you may be mature and complete, not lacking anything. If any of you lacks wisdom, you should ask God, who gives generously to all without finding fault, and it will be given to you." (James 1:2–5)

Like wheat when threshed to separate what is useful, God will use trials that come our way to purify us and pull out what is bad. Daniel was devoted to the Lord and so were his friends. He was thrown into the lion's den for praying to God. Daniel stayed devoted, and God brought Him through miraculously. "The royal administrators, prefects, satraps, advisers, and governors have all agreed that the king should issue an edict and enforce the decree that anyone who prays to any god or human being during the next thirty days, except to you, Your Majesty, shall be thrown into the lions' den." (Daniel 6:7)

"So the king gave the order, and they brought Daniel and threw Him into the lions' den. The king said to Daniel, "May your God, whom you serve continually, rescue you!" A stone was brought and placed over the mouth of the den, and the king sealed it with his own signet ring and with the rings of his nobles so that Daniel's situation might not be changed. Then the king returned to his palace and spent the night without eating and without any entertainment being brought to Him. And he could not sleep. At the first light of dawn, the king got up and hurried to the lions' den. When he came near the den, he called to Daniel in an anguished voice, "Daniel, servant of the living God, has your God, whom you serve continually, been able to rescue you from the lions?" Daniel answered, "May the king live forever! My God sent his angel and He shut the mouths of the lions. They have not hurt me because I was found innocent in His sight. Nor have I ever done any wrong before you, Your Majesty." The king was overjoyed and gave orders to lift Daniel out of the den. And when Daniel was lifted from the den, no wound was found on Him, because he had trusted in his God. At the king's

command, the men who had falsely accused Daniel were brought in and thrown into the lions' den, along with their wives and children. And before they reached the floor of the den, the lions overpowered them and crushed all their bones. Then King Darius wrote to all the nations and peoples of every language in all the earth: "May you prosper greatly! "I issue a decree that in every part of my kingdom, people must fear and reverence the God of Daniel." (Daniel 6:16–26)

Depending on how receptive you are to learning and receiving correction, the trials that you go through may be long or short, and they are only meant to purify your heart. "These have come so that the proven genuineness of your faith—of greater worth than gold, which perishes even though refined by fire—may result in praise, glory, and honor when Jesus Christ is revealed." (1 Peter 1:7)

Sin will keep your heart bound, restless, heavy, and with no peace. Jesus died to give you peace! "Peace I leave with you; my peace I give you. I do not give to you as the world gives. Do not let your hearts be troubled and do not be afraid." (John 14:27)

Rebellion—not wanting to own up to the fact that maybe there are areas within that you need to change, choices you have made that may have been wrong, and sin you may have committed and not repented will only create a path and a doorway into your heart and mind for the enemy to enter and gain control. Hasn't he created enough trouble for you without you helping him to create more?

"In your anger do not sin": Do not let the sun go down while you are still angry and do not give the devil a foothold. Anyone who has been stealing must steal no longer but must work, doing something useful with their own hands, so that they may have something to share with those in need. Do not let any unwholesome talk come out of your mouths, but only what is helpful for building others up according to their needs, that it may benefit those who listen. And do not grieve the Holy Spirit of God, with whom you

were sealed for the day of redemption. Get rid of all bitterness, rage and anger, brawling and slander, along with every form of malice. Be kind and compassionate to one another, forgiving each other, just as in Christ God forgave you." (Ephesians 4:26–32)

That is why this chapter is necessary. As long as you give the enemy access, it will prolong your healing and keep you down and not realize your value in Christ. When King David sought someone from the house of Saul to show kindness, he was led to Mephibosheth who lived in Lo-Debar, living below where God had intended. He was royalty, and he did not even know it and responded. "What is your servant, that you should notice a dead dog like me?" (2 Samuel 9:8)

The Hebrew meaning of Lo-Debar is "pasture less or having no place." We are royalty through Jesus Christ, and God wants us to know it, believe it, and live it! "But you are a chosen people, a royal priesthood, a holy nation, God's special possession, that you may declare the praises of Him who called you out of darkness into his wonderful light." (1 Peter 2:9)

Mephibosheth did not ask for David to find Him; it was the desire of David's heart just as God desires to heal you. "The Lord will restore the splendor of Jacob like the splendor of Israel, though destroyers have laid them waste and have ruined their vines." (Nahum 2:2)

God does not want you living in Lo-Debar, which is probably why you are reading this book. Listen to the Holy Spirit speak to your heart as you read and allow Him to guide you in the steps you need to take.

When Shadrach, Meshach, and Abednego were thrown into the fiery furnace for worshiping God and not the image of Nebuchadnezzar, it was turned up seven times hotter because they would not fall down and worship another god but God Almighty. They stood their ground and stayed faithful to God and not a hair on their head was singed.

"Then King Nebuchadnezzar leaped to his feet in amazement and asked his advisers, "Weren't there three men that we tied up and threw into the fire?" They replied, "Certainly, you're Majesty." He said, "Look! I see four men walking around in the fire, unbound and unharmed, and the fourth looks like a son of the gods." (Daniel 3:24–25)

Their obedience and faith in God not only kept them from being burned but it witnessed to those who saw and they were promoted to the palace. "Then Nebuchadnezzar said, "Praise be to the God of Shadrach, Meshach, and Abednego, who has sent his angel and rescued his servants! They trusted in Him and defied the king's command and were willing to give up their lives rather than serve or worship any god except their own God. Therefore, I decree that the people of any nation or language who say anything against the God of Shadrach, Meshach, and Abednego be cut into pieces and their houses be turned into piles of rubble, for no other god can save in this way." Then the king promoted Shadrach, Meshach, and Abednego in the province of Babylon." (Daniel 3:28–30)

The threshing floor or furnace and trials in your life may feel as if it has been turned up seven times hotter. Satan will not go easy on you, and when you seem to be making progress, he will turn up the heat to make you give up but do not give up. Trust in God and rely on Him; go to Him in prayer, and He will help. God will use these trials to clean out the impurities or that part of our human nature and worldly ways that cannot be used for the kingdom of God just like the wheat on the threshing floor. "Create in me a pure heart, O God, and renew a steadfast spirit within me." (Psalms 51:10) Just use the example of Daniel and his friends and remember how miraculously God brought them through.

God used Malkijah—who was a wrongdoer or sinner and is not said exactly what he did, just that he was a restored wrongdoer—to rebuild the tower of ovens, and it shows God's mercy and forgiveness to let us begin again. God can use anyone anywhere to help and to make a difference. There is always hope for a new beginning in Christ.

"Brothers and sisters, think of what you were when you were called. Not many of you were wise by human standards; not many were influential; not many were of noble birth. But God chose the foolish things of the world to shame the wise; God chose the weak things of the world to shame the strong. God chose the lowly things of this world and the despised things—and the things that are not—to nullify the things that are, so that no one may boast before Him. It is because of Him that you are in Christ Jesus, who has become for us wisdom from God—that is, our righteousness, holiness, and redemption. Therefore, as it is written: "Let the one who boasts boast in the Lord." (1 Corinthians 1:26–31) It shows that God wants to heal and restore and He wants to do the same for you.

It is most proper that the tower of ovens—trials— come before the Valley Gate, a place of humility, and the Dung Gate, a place of cleansing. Through trials, you come to a place of humility and submit to God who upon your repentance cleanses your heart and fills you with his Holy Spirit, which is symbolized by the Fountain Gate, the pool (or king's Pool), and the king's garden that enables the river and power of his Holy Spirit to flow from within you filling you with his fruit, his gifts, and his power to help you become his light to the world. "You are the light of the world. A city on a hill cannot be hidden. Neither do people light a lamp and put it under a bowl. Instead, they put it on its stand, and it gives light to everyone in the house. In the same way, let your light shine before men, that they may see your good deeds and praise your Father in heaven." (Matthew. 5:14–16)

As long as you trust God, pray to and rely on Him, He will bring you safely and victoriously through each trial, and your heart will be totally healed. You will be amazed at the peace and joy that will begin to fill your heart and the new direction God will lead you in life.

"The salvation of the righteous comes from the Lord; He is their

stronghold in times of trouble. The Lord helps them and delivers them; He delivers them from the wicked and saves them because they take refuge in Him." (Psalms 37:39–40)

4

～

New Mortar

Up to now, we have discussed the importance of discovering where the cracks and the brokenness began in order for your heart to have a sure foundation. Going back to each instance and allowing God to go through it with you is vital. If there is one event or person who hurt you and is not completely given over to God, then it will arise later causing you pain— pain in which you are trying to be delivered from and heart healed. When you install ceramic tile on a floor, you put what is called durock, which is a cement board, down first. To do it properly, you must make sure that the floor beneath is swept clean and all spots of glue or other substances are removed to have a completely level floor to work with then you can lay the durock. If you do not clean it properly, then at some point, what is left behind will cause the tile to move and come up. When you allow God to walk with you replacing the darkness of your pain and bitterness with the light of God's love, Jesus, He will heal you and make you whole.

By now I am sure you are learning that you must do your part. Jesus is our sure foundation, and He will create one in your heart if you allow Him. "Nevertheless, God's solid foundation stands firm, sealed with this inscription: 'The Lord knows those who are His,' and, 'Everyone who confesses the name of the Lord must turn away from wickedness'" (2

Timothy 2:19). But He will not go beyond your will. He will not force Himself on you.

"Take my yoke upon you and learn from me, for I am gentle and humble in heart, and you will find rest for your souls." (Matthew. 11:29)

The Lord will not take what you will not give Him, and this leads us to the next gate—the Valley Gate, which is a place of humility. Pride will always lead you astray, away from God, and will keep you from receiving from Him. When people have been hurt so much, they tend to go into protection mode and walls go up. These are self-made walls that God needs to tear down in order to raise his walls—his walls of healing and wholeness. These self-made walls will keep the love of God flowing through your heart in order to restore healing. These are walls of pride, rebellion, bitterness, resentment, anger, and the inability to forgive. These emotions are like mold in a house when left alone will spread and infect the whole house and those who live in it. They say, "No one will ever hurt me again" and, "No one will ever control me again."

These walls are raised up to protect you from getting hurt, and the problem with that is they not only keep others at a distance and from getting through, but they keep God at a distance as well. If you had been very intimate and close to God and have these types of walls built up around your heart, then take a good look at yourself and your relationship with God. Ask yourself, "Have I been as close to God as I once was, and do I worship Him the way I used to?" If the answer to those questions is no, then you have some walls that need to be torn down. "If the defiling mold reappears in the house after the stones have been torn out and the house scraped and plastered, the priest is to go and examine it and, if the mold has spread in the house, it is a persistent defiling mold; the house is unclean. It must be torn down—its stones, timbers, and all the plaster—and taken out of the town to an unclean place." (Leviticus 14:43–45)

It is only through humility that the Lord can come in and heal you and make you whole again. "Pride goes before destruction, a haughty spirit before a fall." (Proverbs 16:18)

The Valley Gate, a place of humility, is where dying to self takes place. You begin to desire to please God more than having your way and your will be done. This is dying to self—you listen to the Holy Spirit that leads you as He speaks to your heart. The previous sections of the Wall and the Valley Gate are in the beginning process of being renewed.

The healing process has begun within your heart and your spirit. Humility is one of the many facets of God's love and the fruit of the Holy Spirit. The Valley Gate is where we can truly learn to walk with God. "The hand of the Lord was on me there, and He said to me, 'Get up and go out to the plain, and there I will speak to you." (Ezekiel 3:22)

The trials we go through will mold us into strong and mature children of God. Jesus was obedient to God, even death on the cross in our place, and that is the greatest showing of love anyone can have. "Greater love has no one than this: to lay down one's life for one's friends." (John 15:13) Upon receiving Jesus into your heart, the fruit of the Spirit is there, and whatever you need, it is already within you. "Flesh gives birth to flesh, but the Spirit gives birth to spirit." (John 3:6)

You have the strength and the power by the Holy Spirit within to over-come, to back down from temptation, to speak boldly for God when you need to, to keep silent when you need to, and to persevere through the most difficult trials. Jesus did it, and with his Spirit within you, you can as well. All you need to do is ask. He is our strength. "I have learned to be content whatever the circumstances. I know what it is to be in need, and I know what it is to have plenty. I have learned the secret of being content in any and every situation, whether well-fed or hungry, whether living in plenty or in want. I can do all this through Him who gives me strength." (Philippians 4:11–13) He is also our joy. "The joy of the Lord is your strength." (Nehemiah 8:10)

We will go down many paths in life that will teach us, correct us, purge us, and draw out of us the spiritual gifts God has given us through the Holy Spirit. "He guides me in paths of righteousness for his name's sake." (Psalms 23:3)

We die more and more each day with each step we take and each lesson learned. We are to walk through and not set up camp and get stuck there. "Even though I walk through the valley of the shadow of death, I will fear no evil, for you are with me." (Psalms 23:4)

The paths you walk are the trials of life that God will use to mold you and transform you. The ways of the world will disappear, and you will be transformed into the child of God He wants you to be. "Consider it pure joy, my brothers, whenever you face trials of many kinds because you know that the testing of your faith develops perseverance. Perseverance must finish its work so that you may be mature and complete, not lacking anything. If any of you lacks wisdom, he should ask God, who gives generously to all without finding fault, and it will be given to him." (James 1:2–5)

The trials you go through will strengthen your faith as you see that your Heavenly Father is there for you and gives you the wisdom and understanding that you need to mature as a Christian and overcome the issues of life. These valleys will weed out the impurities, wrong mindsets, and sinful ways and will purify your heart. "Create in me a pure heart, O God, and renew a steadfast spirit within me. Do not cast me from your presence or take your Holy Spirit from me. Restore to me the joy of your salvation and grant me a willing spirit, to sustain me." (Psalms 51:10–12)

We learn who God is and who we are in Him. "Once you were not a people, but now you are the people of God; once you had not received mercy, but now you have received mercy." (1 Peter 2:10)

We learn humility and the blessings that come as a result. It helps us to be a better person and to grow as a child of God into maturity. When humility is a part of who we are and not what we are trying to achieve in ourselves, the Holy Spirit will flow from within us, out to a lost and dying world. "For the Lord your God is bringing you into a good land—a land with streams and pools of water, with springs flowing in the valleys and hills." (Deuteronomy 8:7)

Jesus came dressed as a servant, not in fine clothes, and a crown on his head. "For you know the grace of our Lord Jesus Christ that though He was rich, yet for your sake He became poor so that you through his poverty might become rich." (2 Corinthians 8:9)

He was led into the desert and was tried and tested so that he could thoroughly understand us. "Since the children have flesh and blood, He too shared in their humanity so that by His death He might destroy Him who holds the power of death—that is, the devil." (Hebrews 2:14)

His humanity helps Him to understand our weaknesses and temptations. "For this reason, He had to be made like his brothers in every way, in order that He might become a merciful and faithful High Priest in service to God, and that He might make atonement for the sins of the people. Because He Himself suffered when He was tempted, He is able to help those who are being tempted." (Hebrews 2:17–18)

Jesus was obedient unto death. He died in our place, putting us first, and God exalted Him. "Your attitude should be the same as that of Christ Jesus: Who being in very nature God; did not consider equality with God something to be grasped, but made Himself nothing, taking the very nature of a servant, being made in human likeness. And being found in appearance as a man, He humbled Himself and became obedient to death, even death on a cross!" (Philippians 2:5–8)

The love of Jesus does not exalt self; it exalts others. "Do nothing out of selfish ambition or vain conceit, but in humility consider others better than yourselves." (Philippians 2:3) He humbled Himself, and God raised Him up. "Therefore God exalted Him to the highest place and gave Him the name that is above every name." (Philippians 2:9)

When we lose our flesh and grow in humility, we learn to be led by the Spirit, and springs of living water will flow from within. "If anyone is thirsty, let Him come to me and drink. Whoever believes in me, as the Scripture has said, streams of living water will flow from within Him." (John 7:38)

We will begin to live in the purpose God has called us to, which is being a "Vessel of his grace." "For we are God's workmanship, created in Christ Jesus to do good works, which God has prepared in advance for us to do." (Ephesians 2:10)

"All authority in heaven and on earth has been given to me. Therefore go and make disciples of all nations, baptizing them in the name of the Father and of the Son and of the Holy Spirit, and teaching them to obey everything I have commanded you. And surely I am with you always, to the very end of the age." (Matthew. 28:17–20)

Jesus is our binding agent, which is what mortar is between bricks. When repairing a foundation, discovering all the cracks, and filling them in with new mortar or concrete, this will make the foundation strong again. As you revisit all the places in your heart where pain resides and the places of sin and allow God to go with you, forgiving and letting go and repenting, the binding agent of God's love through Jesus Christ will be like mortar to your heart. Healing and a fresh cleansing will take place. He is who holds all things together. "He is before all things, and in Him all things hold together." (Colossians 1:17)

Jesus gives us new hope and joy. "May the God of hope fill you with all joy and peace as you trust in Him, so that you may overflow with hope by the power of the Holy Spirit." (Romans 15:13)

This leads us to the next part of the wall—the Dung Gate. Dung comes from ashpoth and means a "heap of rubbish or filth." The Dung Gate is a place of cleansing. It represents the cleansing of our souls through Jesus Christ. It is a place where we take our sins to Jesus and nail them to the cross. When we repent and give our hearts, pain, sin, and all completely over to God in humility, revering Him as our one true God. He "Takes the trash out," so to speak and cleansing takes place in your heart.

"When you were dead in your sins and in the uncircumcision of your sinful nature, God made you alive with Christ. He forgave us all our sins, having canceled the written code, with its regulations, that was against us and that stood opposed to us; He took it away, nailing it to the cross. And having disarmed the powers and authorities, He made a public spectacle of them, triumphing over them by the cross." (Colossians 2:13–15)

The Dung Gate was located near the Pool of Siloam and near the Valley of Hinnom, where refuse (waste) was taken to be burned. The Dung Gate, being located near a place where trash/waste is burned, is quite appropriate. Jesus healed a blind man by spitting on the ground and making mud and putting it on the man's eyes. He told Him to wash in the Pool of Siloam, and when he obeyed, he could see again! Jesus, who created all things, put mud from the dirt—the ground in which He created in the beginning, on the man's eyes to make them new as it was in the beginning. "For in Him all things were created: things in heaven and on earth, visible and invisible, whether thrones or powers or rulers or authorities; all things have been created through Him and for Him." (Colossians 1:16)

When our eyes are finally opened to the light of Christ and we become aware that we need salvation, we take our sins to Jesus and ask for forgiveness and ask Him into our hearts. Our souls are purified through the blood He shed on the cross, and we have a new beginning, a fresh start, and a fresh new heart. "But if we walk in the light, as He is in the light, we have fellowship with one another, and the blood of Jesus, his Son, purifies us from all sin." (1 John 1:7)

"And through Him to reconcile to Himself all things, whether things on earth or things in heaven, by making peace through his blood, shed on the cross." (Colossians 1:20) Just as the waste brought to the Valley of Hinnom to be disposed of, our Lord does the same for us regarding our sins. It is the work of sanctification through Jesus Christ. Our sins are erased and remembered no more, and our hearts and souls are purified. "For I will forgive their wickedness and remember their sins no more." (Hebrews 8:12)

We get a brand new start and the ability to have all the bad choices we made in the past eradicated and forgotten. Praise God for his never-ending love and his wonderful gift to mankind! "Therefore, if anyone is in Christ, he is a new creation; the old has gone, the new has come!"(2 Corinthians 5:17). It is by the overwhelming love, grace, and mercy of God that in his love He corrects, disciplines, comforts, provides, protects, delivers, heals, and saves you.

When Cyrus overthrew Babylon, it was through God changing his heart to want to encourage his subjects that He allowed fifty thousand Jews to return home under the leadership of Zerubbabel. When you let Jesus into your heart and each painful situation past and present, the healing rain of his love will cleanse and heal your heart. "At one time we too were foolish, disobedient, deceived, and enslaved by all kinds of passions and pleasures. We lived in malice and envy, being hated and hating one another. But when the kindness and love of God our Savior appeared, He saved us, not because of righteous things we had done, but because of his mercy. He saved us through the washing of rebirth and renewal by the Holy Spirit, whom He poured out on us generously through Jesus Christ our Savior, so that, having been justified by his grace, we might become heirs having the hope of eternal life." (Titus 3:3–7)

In the cleansing process, you must do it God's way. In the book of Ezra, when King Cyrus allowed the Jews to come back to Jerusalem to repair the temple, they discarded the trash and the rubble and chose to trust God again and worship Him. Without trust and faith that He will heal you, everything you do will be useless if you do not believe that He will. "And without faith, it is impossible to please God, because anyone who comes to Him must believe that He exists and that He rewards those who earnestly seek Him." (Hebrews 11:6)

The Jews assembled as one. There must be unity and no division. Division only creates an open door for the enemy to come in and tear down and destroy you, your family, and your relationships. "How good and pleasant it is when God's people live together in unity! It is like precious oil poured on the head, running down on the beard, running down on Aaron's beard, down on the collar of his robe. It is as if the dew of Hermon were falling on Mount Zion. For there the Lord bestows his blessing, even life forevermore." (Psalms 133)

The destruction the enemy will cause due to division and discord is the exact thing you are trying to be delivered from and replaced with restoration. The Jews assembled and prayed and gave thanks to God. God inhabits the praises of his people. "But thou art holy, O thou that inhabits the praises of Israel." (Psalms 22:3)

And where He is, there is liberty and victory! "Rejoice always, pray continually, give thanks in all circumstances; for this is God's will for you in Christ Jesus." (1 Thessalonians 5:16–18)

"May the peoples praise you, God; may all the peoples praise you. The land yields its harvest; God, our God, blesses us. May God bless us still, so that all the ends of the earth will fear Him." (Psalms 67:5–7)

The Israelites began to lay a new foundation, and right now if you are following along in your heart as you read, you are at a place to do the same thing. They got rid of the trash and set it into their hearts to persevere and begin the work. If you do not start, you will not finish! Now is the time! Get started! Jesus is waiting and wants to heal you. "For He says, "In the time of my favor I heard you, and in the day of salvation I helped you." I tell you, now is the time of God's favor, now is the day of salvation." (2 Corinthians 6:2)

The new mortar of God's love, peace, and joy will make your heart strong again. The more you learn from God's way of doing things and reap its rewards, the stronger you will get, and the more faith you will have. "Tell the righteous it will be well with them, for they will enjoy the fruit of their deeds." (Isaiah 3:10)

The Dung Gate was located near the Pool of Siloam— and how fitting— at the Pool of Siloam is where Jesus spread mud over the blind man's eyes and told Him to wash in the Pool of Siloam; he could see again once he obeyed. When we obey and follow Jesus, the eyes of our hearts will be opened, and we will understand the Word of God and be able to follow God's instructions for us within it. Our eyes will also be opened to the truth and the truth behind every lie the enemy has told us.

"I keep asking that the God of our Lord Jesus Christ, the glorious Father, may give you the Spirit of wisdom and revelation, so that you may know Him better. I pray that the eyes of your heart may be enlightened in order that you may know the hope to which He has called you, the riches of His glorious inheritance in His holy people and His incomparably great power for us who believe. That power is the same as the mighty strength He exerted when He raised Christ from the dead and seated Him at his right hand in the heavenly realms, far above all rule and authority, power and dominion, and every name that is invoked, not only in the present age but also in the one to come. And God placed all things under his feet and appointed Him

to be head over everything for the church, which is his body, the fullness of Him who fills everything in every way." (Ephesians 1:17–23)

Just like the blind man received his miracle, when you allow Jesus to cleanse your heart and soul and take your pain, doing it his way, a miracle will happen in your heart. A sure foundation will fill the cracks in your heart, and joy will be birthed!

"So this is what the Sovereign Lord says: "See, I lay a stone in Zion, a tested stone, a precious cornerstone for a sure foundation; the one who relies on it will never be stricken with panic." (Isaiah 28:16)

Part 3: Repairer Of Broken Walls

"You will be called Repairer of Broken Walls."

5

~

Raise Up New Walls

I hope by now you are learning how important it is to let go and to hand it all over to God. It is also important to your joy and peace to forgive and to seek forgiveness, to humble yourself and allow God to cleanse your heart. These steps will close the door of your heart to the enemy. The result is clearing an open path for the healing rain of God's love to flow through your heart.

Part of repairing the walls of a building is tearing down damaged ones and raising up stronger ones. In this chapter, we are going to look at what it means to raise up new walls in your heart, fortified with God's love and power. "But the Lord has become my fortress, and my God the rock in whom I take refuge." (Psalms 94:22) As the Lord put it, "You cannot pour new wine into old wineskins."

"And no one pours new wine into old wineskins. Otherwise, the wine will burst the skins, and both the wine and the wineskins will be ruined. No, they pour new wine into new wineskins." (Mark 2:22)

Replacing the damaged parts of your heart with new ones through the love, grace, mercy, and forgiveness of God through Jesus Christ will revive your heart. "For every house is built by someone, but God is the builder of everything." (Hebrews 3:4)

In allowing Him into every part of you, including the closed-off places due to heartache, you are becoming one with the Father and stronger through the Trinity—Father, Son, and Holy Spirit. "For we are co-workers in God's service; you are God's field, God's building." (1 Corinthians 3:9) "Don't you know that you yourselves are God's temple and that God's Spirit dwells in your midst?" (1 Corinthians 3:16)

The fullness of God is in Christ, and with Christ in you, God's fullness is in you. Through Jesus Christ and his Holy Spirit, you are a mighty fortress. "For in Christ all the fullness of the Deity lives in bodily form, and in Christ you have been brought to fullness." (Colossians 2:9–10)

To grow in Christ and become spiritually stronger, you must stay in the Word. It is vital to your spiritual health, as food is to your body. Jesus is "the Word, who became flesh" and says, "I am the bread of life." In allowing the Jews to return home, King Cyrus ordered Ezra to teach the Word. In constructing and building anything, you need instructions or plans. The Bible is your instructions on how to live a victorious life in God's way. It is the power of God as spoken into the hearts of men and given to you and me. Read it, study it, and speak it! "For Ezra had devoted Himself to the study and observance of the Law of the Lord, and to teaching its decrees and laws in Israel." (Ezra 7:10)

There is power in the Word! God created the world with his spoken Word. "And God said, "Let there be light," and there was light." (Genesis 1:3)

God's Word spoken through you and me is still his Word and is still just as powerful because it is his Word—it is life. "The Spirit gives life; the flesh counts for nothing. The words I have spoken to you—they are full of the Spirit and life." (John 6:63)

God sends out His Word and achieves his purpose, and with his Spirit in you, it will do the same. "As the rain and the snow come down from heaven, and do not return to it without watering the earth and making it bud and flourish, so that it yields seed for the sower and bread for the eater, so is my word that goes out from my mouth: It will not return to me empty but will accomplish what I desire and achieve the purpose for which I sent it. You will go out in joy and be led forth in peace; the mountains and hills will burst into song before you, and all the trees of the field will clap their hands. Instead of the thorn bush will grow the juniper, and instead of briers, the myrtle will grow. This will be for the Lord's renown, for an everlasting sign that will endure forever." (Isaiah 55:10–13)

To have an effect, you must read the Word in order to know it and all the promises within and in order to speak and declare those promises over your life and each situation that arises. "The tongue has the power of life and death, and those who love it will eat its fruit." (Proverbs 18:21)

You can create your world with your words through faith in God's love and promises. Just what kind of world you create is up to you and the words that you speak. Speak doom and gloom, worry and fear, "I never" or "God won't," and that is what you will receive. When you speak out in this way, you not only destroy your own hope but you give the enemy ammunition. Doesn't he already have enough without you helping Him? He hears what you speak, but He cannot read your mind. Stop speaking out the fears you have, instead take them to God in prayer. Speak words of faith, and you will keep your heart full of hope and will receive blessings and answered prayers. As you speak God's Word, your heart hears, and your faith grows as well, and you grow even stronger spiritually. It is a win-win situation. "So then faith comes by hearing, and hearing by the Word of God." (Romans 10:17)

When you speak the Word, it will have a two-fold effect—your faith grows, and God creates a better world for you through your faith and the power behind his Words. When Jesus was taken into the desert to be tested, He used the Word of God against Satan. This is a must to stand because Satan knows his destiny and wants to destroy and take as many of God's creation with him as he can. "The thief comes only to steal and kill and destroy; I have come that they may have life, and have it to the full." (John 10:10)

Satan used scare tactics to stop rebuilding the wall, but Nehemiah did not fall for it! The Israelites kept working armed with swords—the Word! "May the praise of God be in their mouths and a double-edged sword in their hands, to inflict vengeance on the nations and punishment on the peoples, to bind their kings with fetters, their nobles with shackles of iron, to carry out the sentence written against them—this is the glory of all his faithful people. Praise the Lord." (Psalms 149:6–9)

He used scare and intimidation tactics against rebuilding the temple. In Ezra chapter 4, the people surrounding Jerusalem conspired and wrote a letter to the king with false accusations, and the rebuilding of the Temple was ordered by force to stop. But God! Satan may try, but he does not win! God always finishes what He starts. "Being confident of this, that He who began a good work in you will carry it on to completion until the day of Christ Jesus" (Philippians 1:6). "My purpose will stand, and I will do all that I please." (Isaiah 46:10)

Haggai and Zechariah, two prophets of God, prophesied to the people and encouraged them. Zerubbabel set out to begin work again. Don't let Satan bully you into giving into fear, doubt, and unbelief. Who are you going to believe— God or Satan? Fear does not come from God, so it must come from Satan.

"The Spirit you received does not make you slaves so that you live in fear again; rather, the Spirit you received brought about your adoption to sonship. And by Him we cry, 'Abba, Father." (Romans 8:15)

Stay in faith, and do not back down, just like Zerubbabel. Are you going to believe Satan, the one who wants to destroy your life or God, the One who wants to save your life and died to give you eternal life?

Satan did not leave it at that. He worked through Tattenai, the governor of Trans-Euphrates, and his associate, Shethar-Bozenai, to make trouble. They wrote a letter to King Darius, but the king issued an order to search the archives and found the order to rebuild the temple issued under King Cyrus, and the temple was rebuilt. "They tunnel through the rock; their eyes see all its treasures. They search the sources of the rivers and bring hidden things to light." (Job 28:10–11)

Our enemy, the devil, just hasn't figured out that God is Creator, Almighty, and All-Powerful and God of all— and he is not! God and his children—we always win! "With God, we will gain the victory, and He will trample down our enemies." (Psalms 60:12)

Don't ever give up on God; He is faithful. "The Lord is faithful to all his promises and loving toward all He has made." (Psalms 145:13)

The healing may take time, but as long as you do not give up on God, you will be healed and your prayers answered! Satan's tactics to stop rebuilding God's temple failed. King Darius even issued a decree that no one should interfere. How that is for God protecting what is his? The Lord changed the attitude of the king's heart, and the temple was finished. "For seven days they celebrated with joy the Festival of Unleavened Bread because the Lord had filled them with joy by changing the attitude of the king of Assyria so that he assisted them in the work on the house of God, the God of Israel." (Ezra 6:22)

You are the temple of God. He will rebuild and restore your heart, and the "river of life "will flow through everything broken and will make you new again. This leads us to the next gate they repaired in the book of Nehemiah—the Fountain Gate.

The Fountain Gate in Hebrew means "eyes," and in the dictionary, it means a "spring of water." A spring is a natural source of living water, and in Palestine, it was a land of brooks of water, fountains, and depths that spring out of valleys and hills. "For the Lord, your God is bringing you into a good land—a land with brooks, streams, and deep springs gushing out into the valleys and hills." (Deuteronomy 8:7) "But the land you are crossing the Jordan to take possession of is a land of mountains and valleys that drinks rain from heaven." (Deuteronomy 11:11)

These fountains, bright sparkling eyes of the desert were remarkable for their abundance and beauty. The Fountain Gate represents the Holy Spirit in which our once dry desert spirit becomes alive and flowing with the river of life—Jesus Christ. The symbolism of the Fountain Gate and its meaning fits so perfectly because it is through Jesus Christ and his Holy Spirit that our eyes are opened and the river of his love flowing through us will heal and restore everything broken in our lives and hearts. "If anyone is thirsty, let Him come to me and drink. Whoever believes in me, as the Scripture has said, streams of living water will flow from within Him." (John 7:38)

Upon receiving Jesus as Lord, you are filled with the Holy Spirit. "Because you are sons, God sent the Spirit of his Son into our hearts, the Spirit who calls out, 'Abba, Father.' So you are no longer a slave, but a son; and since you are a son, God has made you also an heir." (Galatians 4:6– 7)—thus being "Born again."

"I tell you the truth; no one can see the kingdom of God unless he is born again." (John 3:3)

We are made alive with Christ in this. "But because of his great love for us, God, who is rich in mercy, made us alive with Christ even when we were dead in transgressions—it is by grace you have been saved." (Ephesians 2:4–5)

The Spirit of the Lord flows from within you like living water. "Everyone who drinks this water will be thirsty again, but whoever drinks the water I give Him will never thirst. Indeed, the water I give Him will become in Him a spring of water welling up to eternal life." (John 4:13–14)

When we receive Jesus as Lord, our eyes are opened— our spiritual eyes —and we have spiritual understanding. "I, the Lord, have called you in righteousness; I will take hold of your hand. I will keep you and will make you to be a covenant for the people and a light for the Gentiles, to open eyes that are blind, to free captives from prison, and to release from the dungeon those who sit in darkness." (Isaiah 42:6–7)

"The fear of the Lord is the beginning of knowledge, but fools despise wisdom and discipline." (Proverbs 1:7)

Upon receiving Jesus as Lord and asking for forgiveness of our sins, we are cleansed and purified. "But if we walk in the light, as He is in the light, we have fellowship with one another, and the blood of Jesus, his Son, purifies us from all sin. If we claim to be without sin, we deceive ourselves and the truth is not in us. If we confess our sins, He is faithful and just and will forgive us our sins and purify us from all unrighteousness." (1 John 1:7–9)

Just as the blind man Jesus healed by putting mud on his eyes, we receive our sight, our spiritual eyesight. "The blind receive sight, the lame walk, those who have leprosy are cured, the deaf hear, the dead are raised, and the good news is preached to the poor." (Matthew. 11:5)

We are then filled with the Holy Spirit. "Then He opened their minds so they could understand the Scriptures. He told them, 'This is what is written: The Christ will suffer and rise from the dead on the third day, and repentance and forgiveness of sins will be preached in his name to all nations, beginning at Jerusalem. You are witnesses of these things. I am going to send you what my Father has promised, but stay in the city until you have been clothed with power from on high." (Luke 24:45–49)

Allowing Jesus into your heart and inviting his Holy Spirit into every part of your life and Spirit will give you a revelation of his truth and love. He will hold your heart together and walk through the process of healing all that is broken in your life and bring glory to God so people who know you may be witnessed to and helped at the same time.

"In the past, God spoke to our ancestors through the prophets at many times and in various ways, but in these last days, He has spoken to us by his Son, whom He appointed heir of all things, and through whom also He made the universe. The Son is the radiance of God's glory and the exact representation of his being, sustaining all things by his powerful Word. After He had provided purification for sins, He sat down at the right hand of the Majesty in heaven. So He became as much superior to the angels as the name He has inherited is superior to theirs." (Hebrews 1:1–4)

6

～

Reinforce The Walls

To make it through life victoriously, staying content and filled with the peace and joy of the Lord, you need God to strengthen your heart.

"Strengthen the feeble hands, steady the knees that give way; say to those with fearful hearts, "Be strong, do not fear; your God will come, He will come with vengeance; with divine retribution, He will come to save you." Then will the eyes of the blind be opened and the ears of the deaf unstopped. Then will the lame leap like a deer and the mute tongue shout for joy. Water will gush forth in the wilderness and streams in the desert. The burning sand will become a pool, the thirsty ground bubbling springs. In the haunts where jackals once lay, grass and reeds, and papyrus will grow. And a highway will be there; it will be called the Way of Holiness; it will be for those who walk on that Way. The unclean will not journey on it; wicked fools will not go about on it. No lion will be there, nor any ravenous beast; they will not be found there. But only the redeemed will walk there, and those the Lord has rescued will return. They will enter Zion with singing; everlasting joy will crown their heads. Gladness and joy will overtake them, and sorrow and sighing will flee away." (Isaiah 35:3–10)

As a new creation in Christ, you need to do things God's way in order to live a victorious life. After all, your way has not worked out too well for you, has it? With the Holy Spirit in your heart, his love fills your heart, and in daily reading of the Word, your spiritual food, God will keep your heart strong and able to endure the attacks of the enemy and overcome them. Without reading the Bible, you will grow weak spiritually, and you will fall. Up to now, the attacks of the enemy and persecution and insults of others have worn you down and broken your heart; depression among other emotions has overwhelmed your heart.

Have you been reading your Bible? If not, then that is part of the reason. Jesus says, "I am the bread of life." He is bread, food for our souls. He is our living Word, which makes our hearts come alive and gives us the fruit of the Spirit, wisdom, and understanding from God and the Bible—the written Word keeps the Spirit alive and strong within us. "Do not quench the Spirit." (1 Thess. 5:19) If you can quench the Spirit, then it can grow weak as well if not fed. Even Jesus withdrew to be alone and talk with the Father, and He was the Son of God! Shouldn't we then do likewise being human and full of weaknesses?

The insults of those who oppose you will have no effect because God's love is so complete within you, that it makes you secure in His love. What others think of you or not does not make a difference. "But He said to me, 'My grace is sufficient for you, for my power is made perfect in weakness.' Therefore, I will boast all the more gladly about my weaknesses so that Christ's power may rest on me. That is why, for Christ's sake, I delight in weaknesses, in insults, in hardships, in persecutions, in difficulties. For when I am weak, then I am strong." (2 Corinthians 12:9–10)
Jesus was ridiculed, insulted, and spit on, and He did not fight back.

"When Jesus came out wearing the crown of thorns and the purple robe, Pilate said to them, "Here is the man!" As soon as the chief priests and their officials saw Him, they shouted, "Crucify! Crucify!" But Pilate answered, "You take Him and crucify him. As for me, I find no basis for a charge against Him." The Jewish leaders insisted, "We have a law, and according

to that law He must die because he claimed to be the Son of God."
When Pilate heard this, he was even more afraid, and he went back inside
the palace. "Where do you come from?" he asked Jesus, but Jesus gave Him
no answer. "Do you refuse to speak to me?" Pilate said. "Don't you realize I
have power either to free you or to crucify you?" Jesus answered, "You would
have no power over me if it were not given to you from above. Therefore, the
one who handed me over to you is guilty of a greater sin." (John 19:5–11)

"For you have been born again, not of perishable seed, but of imperishable,
through the living and enduring word of God. For, 'All people are like grass,
and all their glory is like the flowers of the field; the grass withers and the
flowers fall, but the Word of the Lord endures forever." (1 Peter 1:23–25)

The Spirit of the Lord within you will help you to do the same. He will
help you to let insults roll right off your back knowing it is just the enemy
trying to trap you into an emotional prison. The same Spirit that was
with Jesus and gave Him power is the same Spirit that will help you because his Spirit is the "same yesterday, today, and forever." Without Him
and his strength working through you, you will get offended easily, heartbroken often, and insecurity will take root in your heart. The insecure
have low self-esteem and look for validation from others, and when they
do not get it, they get hurt easily. When you are secure in yourself and in
knowing God loves you, what others think of you or not will not matter.
God wants your confidence to be in Christ and come from Him knowing
who you are and whose you are and knowing your value is found only in
Jesus Christ who will "never leave you nor forsake you."

Your value is in a love so great, that He died for you. People are flesh and
"the flesh is weak" and will purposely or not at one time or another fail
you. God never will. "For we all fall short of the glory of God." (Romans
3:23) When your confidence is in Christ and your value comes from
Him, then the opinions of others will not matter to you.

To live a victorious life, you need Jesus and his Holy Spirit. Without Him, you can expect the woes of life to hit and failure to follow. "I am the vine; you are the branches. If you remain in me and me in you, you will bear much fruit; apart from me you can do nothing." (John 15:5)

We receive the fruit of the Spirit through the Holy Spirit when we ask Jesus into our hearts. This leads us to the next part of the wall—the wall near the Pool of Siloam. "Then I moved on toward the Fountain Gate and the King's Pool, but there was not enough room for my mount to get through." (Nehemiah 2:14)

"The Fountain Gate was repaired by Shallun, son of Kol-Hozeh, ruler of the district of Mizpah. He rebuilt it, roofing it over and putting its doors and bolts and bars in place. He also repaired the wall of the Pool of Siloam, by the King's Garden, as far as the steps going down from the City of David." (Nehemiah 3:15) Pool, as said before, is from the Hebrew origin Barak meaning "reservoir," and Barak means "abundantly blessed." God wants to abundantly bless us, and He has a pool or reservoir of blessings stored up for us. "The thief cometh not, but for to steal, and to kill, and to destroy: I have come that they might have life and that they might have it more abundantly." (John 10:10)

Rubble and too much of it from the broken wall made it impossible for Nehemiah and his horse to get through the Fountain Gate, which was prophesied by Jeremiah years before. "Zion will be plowed like a field, Jerusalem will become a heap of rubble, the temple hill a mound overgrown with thickets." (Jeremiah 26:18)

The Fountain Gate symbolizes the Holy Spirit and the flow of his fruit. Siloam is from the Greek and means "sent" or "gushing forth." So from the Holy Spirit, his fruit should "gush forth" from us to the world. It should be seen in us first, without having to say we are Christians. It should be evident by our fruit. "Whoever believes in me, as Scripture has said, rivers of living water will flow from within them." (John 7:38)— and the king's pool, which symbolizes the fruit of the Spirit.

When we choose our own way instead of submitting to His and when we let offense and abuse of others settle into our hearts without giving it over to Him to take care of, it creates more rubble in our hearts. It creates an idol in your heart when you place your own will above God's, and it creates emotions that weigh your heart down such as bitterness, resentment, the inability to forgive, and more. These will grow as trees with roots in our hearts. The longer you leave them in your heart, to more branches it grows such as anger, frustration, doubt, etc.

This creates more rubble and eventually leads you astray, away from God, and it blocks any room for the fruit of the Spirit to grow in your heart. Giving everything over to God and following God's book of instructions, the Bible, and staying close to Him through daily fellowship, the fruit of the Spirit will increase and flow from within you.

Besides the fruit of the Spirit, we also receive gifts of the Spirit from the Holy Spirit, and this too is vital to our spiritual growth and service to the Lord. This leads us to the next part of the wall. The wall that was repaired by the king's garden, and the king's garden symbolizes the fruit and the gifts.

"Now about the gifts of the Spirit, brothers and sisters, I do not want you to be uninformed. You know that when you were pagans, somehow or other you were influenced and led astray to mute idols. Therefore, I want you to know that no one who is speaking by the Spirit of God says, "Jesus be cursed," and no one can say, "Jesus is Lord," except by the Holy Spirit. There are different kinds of gifts, but the same Spirit distributes them. There are different kinds of service, but the same Lord. There are different kinds of working, but in all of them and in everyone it is the same God at work.
Now to each one, the manifestation of the Spirit is given for the common good. To one there is given through the Spirit a message of wisdom, to another a message of knowledge by means of the same Spirit, to another faith by the same Spirit, to another gifts of healing by that one Spirit, to

another miraculous powers, to another prophecy, to another distinguishing between spirits, to another speaking in different kinds of tongues, and to still another the interpretation of tongues. All these are the work of one and the same Spirit, and He distributes them to each one, just as He determines." (1 Corinthians 12:1–11)

The gifts of the Holy of the Spirit, are planted in your heart as a seed and need the watering of the Word, time spent with God in prayer and worship, and obedience to God in order to grow. "But the fruit of the Spirit is love, joy, peace, forbearance, kindness, goodness, faithfulness, gentleness, and self-control. Against such things, there is no law. Those who belong to Christ Jesus have crucified the flesh with its passions and desires. Since we live by the Spirit, let us keep in step with the Spirit. Let us not become conceited, provoking, and envying each other." (Galatians 5:22–26)

Like weeds in a garden, sin, and offenses that create hurt and bitter feelings that are not repented of and emotions given over to God will create rubble in your heart, and like weeds, it will consume your heart and will cause a block and quench the Holy Spirit and the gifts. "Do not quench the Spirit." (1 Thessalonians 5:19)

God wants to pull those weeds, but you must let Him; He will not go against your will. "Every plant that my heavenly Father has not planted will be pulled up by the roots." (Matthew. 15:13)

Choose to forgive and repent of unconfessed sin and give all over to God to deal with. "Do not repay anyone evil for evil. Be careful to do what is right in the eyes of everyone. If it is possible, as far as it depends on you, live at peace with everyone. Do not take revenge, my dear friends, but leave room for God's wrath, for it is written: 'It is mine to avenge; I will repay,' says the Lord." (Romans 12:17–19)

Repent and God will forgive. "Therefore I tell you, whatever you ask for in prayer, believe that you have received it, and it will be yours. And when you stand praying, if you hold anything against anyone, forgive them, so that your Father in heaven may forgive you your sins. But if you do not forgive, neither will your Father who is in heaven forgive your transgressions." (Mark 11:24–26) "But if we walk in the light, as He is in the light, we have fellowship with one another, and the blood of Jesus, his Son, purifies us from all sin. If we claim to be without sin, we deceive ourselves and the truth is not in us. If we confess our sins, He is faithful and just and will forgive us our sins and purify us from all unrighteousness." (1 John 1:7–9)

In doing this, God cleanses and purifies your heart, the weeds and rubble removed. "Create in me a pure heart, O God, and renew a steadfast spirit within me." (Psalms 51:10)

Nehemiah had to enter through the Valley Gate, which symbolizes humility. It is in humility that we surrender, admit our sins, and repent. "But He gives us more grace. That is why Scripture says: 'God opposes the proud but shows favor to the humble.' Submit yourselves, then, to God. Resist the devil, and he will flee from you. Come near to God and He will come near to you." (James 4:6–8)

When you forgive and let go, God will pull the weeds clearing a path for the fruit of the Spirit and the gifts He wants to bestow on you to grow and flourish in your heart, and once again the joy of your salvation will be restored creating an awesome testimony in the process that will speak of itself to all who know you. "Restore to me the joy of your salvation and grant me a willing spirit, to sustain me." (Psalms 51:12)

When Nehemiah went to the people and told them the plan God had placed in his heart to rebuild the wall of Jerusalem, the work of repairing the wall began, just as God will heal and restore your heart when you go to Him for help.

God has a reservoir of blessings and joy stored up for you; don't block the path to receive them! God's gift, the Holy Spirit, and the fruit and gifts that come from his Spirit are what allow us to live victorious Christian lives. When you step away and allow yourself to get caught up in the world, rubble will start to build. "They all plotted together to come and fight against Jerusalem and stir up trouble against it. But we prayed to our God and posted a guard day and night to meet this threat. Meanwhile, the people in Judah said, 'The strength of the laborers is giving out, and there is so much rubble that we cannot rebuild the wall." (Nehemiah 4: 8–10)

Your strength will depart making a way for Satan to attack. Stay on guard! Guard your heart daily, and allow God to clear the way! "Praise be to the God and Father of our Lord Jesus Christ, who has blessed us in the heavenly realms with every spiritual blessing in Christ." (Ephesians 1:3)

The fruit and the gifts of the Holy Spirit are tools needed to keep you strong and able to withstand Satan's attacks. When Nehemiah and the Israelites who were helping Him started repairing the wall, opposition arose. You must remember there is evil in the world and not everyone chooses to follow God. This affords Satan the opportunity to use them in attacking God's children and the work they are doing for Him. This is what happened to Nehemiah. Sanballat, who represents the enemy, was used by Satan to try to stop Nehemiah from repairing the wall. They had to post people with swords at the repair sites. When the enemy was spotted, they would sound trumpets.

What trumpets do we have when discouraging thoughts come into our minds or people or issues arise to overwhelm us or come against us? What trumpets do we have when people do or say hurtful things or when bills surround and overwhelm all at once? Don't fall into the old habit of worrying and getting discouraged! Use your trumpet, your mouth, your heart, and your Bible! Use your mouth to pray and your heart to stand firm. Cry out to God, and use your Bible to find God's promises to speak and to pray, and most of all, use your mouth to continue to praise! "The

name of the Lord is a fortified tower; the righteous run to it and are safe."
(Proverbs 18:10)

Satan will not stick around and praise God with you! "God is our refuge
and strength, an ever-present help in trouble." (Psalms 46:1)

The Bible is our most important trumpet. God exalts his Word. "I will
bow down toward your holy temple and will praise your Name for your
unfailing love and your faithfulness, for you have exalted above all things
your Name and your Word." (Psalms 138:2)

He created the world and all living things by his powerful Word, and
the Bible is his written Word as spoken into the hearts of men. "All Scripture is God-breathed and is useful for teaching, rebuking, correcting and
training in righteousness, so that the servant of God may be thoroughly
equipped for every good work." (2 Timothy 3:16–17).

God exalts His Word, and it accomplishes what it has set out to do. Read
it, speak it, hear it, and get it into your heart. It will transform your mind
and your life. "Therefore, I urge you, brothers and sisters, in view of
God's mercy, to offer your bodies as a living sacrifice, holy and pleasing
to God—this is your true and proper worship. Do not conform to the
pattern of this world, but be transformed by the renewing of your mind.
Then you will be able to test and approve what God's will is—His good,
pleasing, and perfect will." (Romans 12:1–2)

It will also increase your faith. "So then faith comes by hearing, and
hearing by the Word of God." (Romans 10:17)

The Holy Spirit within you will remind you of the Word and the Scriptures you need when you need them, but in order for Him to remind
you, you need to read them first. "But the Comforter, which is the Holy
Ghost, whom the Father will send in my Name, He shall teach you all
things, and bring all things to your remembrance, whatsoever I have said

unto you." (John 14:26) God did not pick the Israelites up and plant them into the Promised Land. They had to walk through the desert and fight battles along the way. That is a symbol of the spiritual warfare we must fight to reach our destiny in Christ and become spiritually mature. You learn through experience, and your faith is grown as a result. In Ezra, the enemy tried to infiltrate the Israelites in order to stop the rebuilding of the temple.

"When the enemies of Judah and Benjamin heard that the exiles were building a temple for the Lord, the God of Israel, they came to Zerubbabel and to the heads of the families and said, "Let us help you build because, like you, we seek your God and have been sacrificing to Him since the time of Esarhaddon king of Assyria, who brought us here." But Zerubbabel, Joshua, and the rest of the heads of the families of Israel answered, "You have no part with us in building a temple to our God. We alone will build it for the Lord, the God of Israel, as King Cyrus, the king of Persia, commanded us." Then the people around them set out to discourage the people of Judah and make them afraid to go on building. They bribed officials to work against them and frustrate their plans during the entire reign of Cyrus king of Persia and down to the reign of Darius king of Persia." (Ezra 4:1–5)

They did not fall for it, but that did not stop Satan. He used their enemies to write a letter to the new king in order to stop the rebuilding. It worked but only temporarily until the rebuilding began again under the direction of Haggai and Zechariah, prophets of God and Zerubbabel. They would not sit like cowards and take it. They served a mighty God, God Almighty, and they knew it and believed and trusted God to back them up if they stepped out in faith to continue the work. God did. He proved Himself faithful to his promise. "I will never leave you nor forsake you," and the work continued, and the rebuilding of the temple was completed. "But blessed is the one who trusts in the Lord, whose confidence is in Him. They will be like a tree planted by the water that sends out its roots by the stream. It does not fear when heat comes; its leaves are always green. It has no worries in a year of drought and never fails to bear fruit." (Jeremiah 17:7–8)

As your heart begins to heal, the enemy is not going to sit by and watch. He will try to create things according to the weaknesses he knows you have and try to destroy and discourage you and your walk in Christ. Beware and be prepared with your trumpet, your mouth, and the Word of God. Don't walk around in fear of the enemy, but stay in daily communion with God, talking to Him and reading the Word. Then when the enemy tries to strike, you are full of the Spirit of the Lord and his strength, and the Holy Spirit will bring the Word that you have already read and put into your spirit to mind when you need it. Use the trumpets you have, your mouth to pray and to praise, and the Word to speak and believe. The Bible, as long as you use it, is the most powerful and effective tool you have as long as you use it. This leads to the next gate—the Water Gate.

The Water Gate is the Word, and Jesus is the Word, who became flesh. "The Word became flesh and made His dwelling among us. We have seen his glory, the glory of the One and only, who came from the Father, full of grace and truth." (John 1:14) He is the bread of life that feeds our souls. "I am the bread of life. He who comes to me will never go hungry, and he who believes in me will never be thirsty." (John 6:35)

Jesus is also our living water that through the Holy Spirit within us, our souls will never thirst again. "If anyone is thirsty, let Him come to me and drink. Whoever believes in me, as the Scripture has said, streams of living water will flow from within Him." (John 7:38)
God's Word was from the beginning. "In the beginning was the Word, and the Word was with God, and the Word was God. He was with God in the beginning." (John 1:1-2)

God spoke, and it came to be. "And God said, 'Let there be light', and there was light." (Genesis 1:3)

His Word is flawless. "Every word of God is flawless; He is a shield to those who take refuge in Him." (Proverbs 30:5) The walls around the Water Gate were repaired, but the Water Gate itself was not. God's Word is flawless and does not need to be fixed. His Word is right the first time, and it stands forever. "The grass withers and the flowers fall, but the Word of our God stands forever." (Isaiah 40:8)

We are to take nothing away from it or add anything to it. "See that you do all I command you; do not add to it or take away from it." (Deuteronomy 12:32)

The Word of God teaches, corrects, and trains. "All Scripture is God-breathed and is useful for teaching, rebuking, correcting and training in righteousness, so that the man of God may be thoroughly equipped for every good work." (2 Timothy 3:16–17)

Through the death of Jesus and receiving Him as Lord, we are filled with the Holy Spirit, and God's Word dwells in us. "Let the Word of Christ dwell in you richly as you teach and admonish one another with all wisdom, and as you sing psalms, hymns, and spiritual songs with gratitude in your hearts to God. And whatever you do, whether in word or deed, do it all in the name of the Lord Jesus, giving thanks to God the Father through Him." (Colossians 3:16–17)

Through the Holy Spirit, the Word sanctifies you. "May God Himself, the God of peace, sanctify you through and through? May your whole spirit, soul and body be kept blameless at the coming of our Lord Jesus Christ" (1 Thessalonians 5:23). "To God's elect, strangers in the world, scattered throughout Pontus, Galatia, Cappadocia, Asia and Bithynia, who have been chosen according to the foreknowledge of God the Father, through the sanctifying work of the Spirit, for obedience to Jesus Christ and sprinkling by his blood: Grace and peace be yours in abundance" (1 Peter 1:1–2). "Sanctify them by the truth; Your Word is truth." (John

17:17)

The more we read and study the Word as we are commanded to do, the more of the Word dwells within us. "Study to show yourself approved unto God, a workman that needs not to be ashamed, rightly dividing the Word of truth." (2 Timothy 2:15) The Lord will teach you and help you to understand. "The fear of the Lord is the beginning of knowledge." (Proverbs 1:7) If you have trouble understanding, all you have to do is ask. "If any of you lacks wisdom, he should ask God, who gives generously to all without finding fault, and it will be given to Him." (James 1:5)

God's Word is living and active; allow Him to make it come alive in you! Ask and you shall receive! "For the Word of God is living and active. Sharper than any double-edged sword, it penetrates even to dividing soul and spirit, joints and marrow; it judges the thoughts and attitudes of the heart." (Hebrews 4:12)

Even in your weakest moments, if you turn to God's Word, God Himself will guide you to a passage of Scripture that will pick you up and lift your spirits. "But those who hope in the Lord will renew their strength. They will soar on wings like eagles; they will run and not grow weary, they will walk and not be faint." (Isaiah 40:31)

The Water Gate rebuilt is the Word firmly planted in your heart. It gives you the effective tools you need to stand firm in your faith and allows God through his Holy Spirit to give you victory. "The Lord said to me, "You have seen correctly, for I am watching to see that my Word is fulfilled." (Jeremiah 1:12)

It also gives the angels something to do! "Are not all angels ministering spirits sent to serve those who will inherit salvation?" (Hebrews 1:14) The Bible, the Word of God, reinforces the walls of your heart, and it will help you to win every battle in life that you face and will help you learn Satan's tactics as well.

The Word firmly planted in your heart will keep it strong, and this will keep the unwanted out! "Draw water for the siege, strengthen your defenses! Work the clay, tread the mortar, and repair the brickwork!" (Nahum 3:14)

It keeps the unwanted out with God's strength and His power working in and through you. You will fail if you continue to try to make it through life on your own. We live in a fallen world in which many people do not fear God or care who they hurt, which is why we need God to go before us and be our rear guard. Without God, Satan will have a free ride in your life. "Yes, and from ancient days I am he. No one can deliver out of my hand. When I act, who can reverse it?" (Isaiah 43:13). "So this is what the Sovereign Lord says: 'See, I lay a stone in Zion, a tested stone, a precious cornerstone for a sure foundation; the one who relies on it will never be stricken with panic." (Isaiah 28:16)

The Word of God renews your mind so you learn to think like God thinks. When you were saved, your heart was made new, but you still had years of the world and old mindsets that needed to be renewed. This is done through walking through your trials with God and learning through experience and growing in faith along the way, as well as daily communion with God and studying the Word of God. "Therefore, I urge you, brothers and sisters, in view of God's mercy, to offer your bodies as a living sacrifice, holy and pleasing to God—this is your true and proper worship. Do not conform to the pattern of this world, but be transformed by the renewing of your mind. Then you will be able to test and approve what God's will is—His good, pleasing, and perfect will." (Romans 12:1–2)

When you allow God to renew your mind and learn his way of thinking and his way of doing things, He will lead you and guide you every step of the way with joy, peace, and victory. "The fruit of that righteousness will be peace; its effect will be quietness and confidence forever. My people will live in peaceful dwelling places, in secure homes, in undisturbed places of rest. Though hail flattens the forest and the city is leveled completely, how blessed you will be, sowing your seed by every stream, and letting your cattle and donkeys range free." (Isaiah 32:17–20)

In the process of trusting God to go through your trials with you—relying on Him, praying to Him, going to Him first for help, and praising Him—the walls of your heart will be reinforced by God and his Word. The walls of your mind and heart will be reinforced with a new confidence in Christ. You will be confident that Christ is in you and confident that "he will never leave you nor forsake you." You will be confident that He is your Savior, Deliverer, Healer, and Restorer. This will help you to be immovable in your faith. "Therefore, my dear brothers and sisters, stand firm. Let nothing move you. Always give yourselves fully to the work of the Lord, because you know that your labor in the Lord is not in vain." (1 Corinthians 15:58)

When you learn and believe and then walk in that belief, knowing who you are in Christ and whose you are, and who you belong to, it will build a wall around your heart and mind that cannot be destroyed—a wall created by the love of God.

"God is our refuge and strength, an ever-present help in trouble. Therefore, we will not fear, though the earth give way and the mountains fall into the heart of the sea, though its waters roar and foam and the mountains quake with their surging. There is a river whose streams make glad the city of God, the holy place where the Most High dwells. God is within her, she will not fall; God will help her at break of day. Nations are in uproar, kingdoms fall; He lifts his voice, and the earth melts. The Lord Almighty is with us; the God of Jacob is our fortress. Come and see what the Lord has done, the desolations He has brought on the earth. He makes wars cease to the ends of the earth. He breaks the bow and shatters the spear; He burns the shields with fire. He says, "Be still, and know that I am God; I will be exalted

among the nations, I will be exalted in the earth." The Lord Almighty is with us; the God of Jacob is our fortress." (Psalms 46)

Part 4: Restorer Of Streets

"Restorer of streets."

7

Pathway Of Hope

If you have been following along and putting into practice what you have learned thus far, then at this stage, your heart is now coming alive again and is being filled with hope more and more as you release each painful event and each person and forgive. The promises of God concerning you are being firmly planted in your heart and mind as you read and meditate on the Word. This helps the hope you have within to be secure and your faith to grow. The hope that you have is a hope for a purpose-filled life blessed by God, hope for family and friends, and hope for your eternal home in heaven. "May the God of hope fill you with all joy and peace as you trust in Him so that you may overflow with hope by the power of the Holy Spirit." (Romans 15:13)

You are beginning to trust God more and more as you continue to draw closer to Him with each part of your heart that is healed. "Lord, by such things people live; and my spirit finds life in them too. You restored me to health and let me live." (Isaiah 38:16)

You have a new confidence within and know that Jesus Christ lives and dwells within you, and you feel his presence rather than the heartache you once had. You know who you are and whose you are—a child of God with hope inside that is alive. "To them, God has chosen to make known among the Gentiles the glorious riches of this mystery, which is Christ in you, the hope of glory." (Colossians 1:27)

New desires are being birthed in your heart. "Take delight in the Lord, and He will give you the desires of your heart" (Psalms 37:4). Like any father, your Heavenly Father wants to bless you with good things—things you want and things you need and desires for things you want to do, but He will also give you desires for the purpose He has for you. "For we are God's handiwork, created in Christ Jesus to do good works, which God prepared in advance for us to do." (Ephesians 2:10)

Now that your heart is not weighed down by the baggage of the past and overwhelming heartache and depression, there is room for the desires and purpose God wants to plant in your heart. "For God has put it into their hearts to accomplish his purpose by agreeing to hand over to the beast their royal authority, until God's words are fulfilled." (Revelations 17:17)

Our life here on earth is temporary, but a breath and our home in heaven is forever.

"A voice says, "Cry out." And I said, "What shall I cry?" "All people are like grass, and all their faithfulness is like the flowers of the field. The grass withers and the flowers fall because the breath of the Lord blows on them. Surely the people are grass. The grass withers and the flowers fall, but the Word of our God endures forever." (Isaiah 40:6–8)

Life on earth is preparation for where we will spend eternity. "For the Lord Himself will come down from heaven, with a loud command, with the voice of the archangel and with the trumpet call of God, and the dead in Christ will rise first. After that, we who are still alive and are left will be caught up together with them in the clouds to meet the Lord in the air. And so we will be with the Lord forever." (1 Thessalonians 4:16–17)

Part of preparing is our continual fellowship with God. When the Israelites finished the repairs, they began praising God, and they renewed their covenant with Him. They rededicated themselves to Him. They repented of their sins and the sins of past generations. Before their exile, as the disobedience and idolatry of the Israelites grew, the reading of the Book of the Law that was commanded of them to do became less and less often until it stopped. This caused them to grow even more and more distant from God. "Keep this Book of the Law always on your lips; meditate on it day and night, so that you may be careful to do everything written in it. Then you will be prosperous and successful. Have I not commanded you? Be strong and courageous. Do not be afraid; do not be discouraged, for the Lord your God will be with you wherever you go." (Joshua 1:8–9)

The Bible is the Word of God, and his Spirit is in his Word. "All Scripture is God-breathed and is useful for teaching, rebuking, correcting and training in righteousness, so that the servant of God may be thoroughly equipped for every good work." (2 Timothy 3:16–17)

When you don't feed on your spiritual food, your spirit will grow weak. The Israelites kept up the acts, the sacrifices, and the festivals, but without the heart—the true devotion behind it—they were just acts. "The Lord says: 'These people come near to me with their mouth and honor me with their lips, but their hearts are far from me. Their worship of me is based on merely human rules they have been taught." (Isaiah 29:13)

I am sure you remember the Tower of Babel, which was an act and trying to get to heaven through human efforts.

"If I speak in the tongues of men or of angels, but do not have love, I am only a resounding gong or a clanging cymbal. If I have the gift of prophecy and can fathom all mysteries and all knowledge, and if I have a faith that can move mountains, but do not have love, I am nothing. If I give all I possess to the poor and give over my body to hardship that I may boast, but do not have love, I gain nothing." (1 Corinthians 13:1–3)

God wants sincere devotion as do we all—works without the heart, without love does not mean anything. "Let us draw near to God with a sincere heart and with the full assurance that faith brings, having our hearts sprinkled to cleanse us from a guilty conscience and having our bodies washed with pure water." (Hebrews 10:22)

The Book of the Law had been lost, which also shows the decay in their relationship with God. If God and his Word meant anything, if they had cherished it, they would not have lost it. But in 640 BC, Josiah became king of Judah in Jerusalem. Not all kings at that time followed God with their whole heart. Josiah, although he was only eight years old, he was truly devoted to God. He wanted to restore the temple, which had been desecrated by Manasseh who was king of Judah in 695–642 BC and who also did evil in the eyes of the Lord. He worshiped Baal and brought idols into the temple and shed innocent blood. When we receive Jesus into our hearts, we become the temple of God. How many of us desecrate it by the idols we ingest (drugs, alcohol, and cigarettes), the things we do with our bodies (pornography, sexual immorality, etc.), and the hate and forgiveness we harbor in our hearts, and then we go to church to worship God as if we had done nothing wrong? Some of us are no different than the Israelites. "Do you not know that your bodies are temples of the Holy Spirit, who is in you, whom you have received from God? You are not your own; you were bought at a price. Therefore honor God with your bodies." (1 Corinthians 6:19–20)

Look at the price He paid, the beatings He endured, the rejection He suffered and still suffers and the cross He hung on for us. How do we repay Him? In making light of sin, we are also making light of his overwhelming unselfish act of love. "Greater love has no one than this: that He lay down his life for his friends." (John 15:13)

Josiah wanted to make things right, so he sent for the high priest, Hilkiah, to collect money to begin repairs. Hilkiah found the Book of the Law, and Josiah was heartbroken at seeing the sin of the people and how great it was as he read it. He made reforms and renewed the covenant, but the sins of the people were too great, and God had already decided to send them into captivity to the Babylonians in order to open their eyes. Judah's sins were just too great, and God—being a loving God and Father—could not let them stay that way. He missed their fellowship just as He misses ours when we stray from Him.

When we sin, it is our own choice, and that choice leads to the consequences of it. It is our own choice to walk away, and God will not bless us when we are living in sin. Sin causes eternal separation, and He loves us too much to let that happen, so He will allow the consequences in order to bring us back to Him. This is why it is said to examine yourself. It is much better to examine yourself and humble yourself and repent than to have to endure a trial to accomplish the same thing. I would much rather do without the trial, wouldn't you? Pride and a stubborn heart will only keep you away from the blessings of God a lot longer than it has to be. "Examine yourselves to see whether you are in the faith; test yourselves. Do you not realize that Christ Jesus is in you—unless, of course, you fail the test?" (2 Corinthians 13:5)

The Bible is our mirror and helps us to see ourselves as God sees us. "Do not merely listen to the Word, and so deceive yourselves. Do what it says. Anyone who listens to the Word but does not do what it says is like someone who looks at his face in a mirror and, after looking at Himself, goes away and immediately forgets what He looks like." (James 1:22–24)

Every parent disciplines out of love to show the child right from wrong, and it is the same with God.

"In your struggle against sin, you have not yet resisted to the point of shedding your blood. And have you completely forgotten this word of encouragement that addresses you as a father addresses his son? It says, "My son, do not make light of the Lord's discipline, and do not lose heart when He rebukes

you, because the Lord disciplines the one He loves, and He chastens everyone He accepts as his son." Endure hardship as discipline; God is treating you as his children. For what children are not disciplined by their fathers? If you are not disciplined—and everyone undergoes discipline —then you are not legitimate, not true sons and daughters at all. Moreover, we have all had human fathers who disciplined us and we respected them for it. How much more should we submit to the Father of spirits and live? They disciplined us for a little while as they thought best; but God disciplines us for our good, so that we may share in his holiness. No discipline seems pleasant at the time, but painful. Later on, however, it produces a harvest of righteousness and peace for those who have been trained by it." (Hebrews 12:4–11)

God wants to bless us, and everything He does or allows is only to lead us to Christ in order to give us eternal life and a home with Him in heaven, to correct us in order to bless us, or to birth a desire and a passion of purpose out of us. "Beloved, I wish above all things that you may prosper and be in health, even as your soul prospers." (3 John 1:2)

Josiah was not led into captivity but was killed in battle. I have to say that I believe that to be mercy on God's part, allowing Him to come into His presence literally rather than being led into captivity. As seen by Israel's and Judah's sins and how it led them into captivity, it was due to their deteriorating relationship with God. When you sin, when you step away thinking, I will do it just this one time or I will skip church this one time or I will start reading the Bible tomorrow, or you stop praying, then your relationship with God will grow cold, and your heart will become callous (hard). It will not be as sensitive to the Holy Spirit as it once was and sin grows and abounds as a result. You give the devil an inch, and He will take it all! "And do not give the devil a foothold." (Ephesians 4:27)

Don't justify, God knows your heart anyway. Just hurry up and humble yourself, and repent and enjoy sweet fellowship with God again. He is waiting! Do you enjoy trials? Not me, they are not fun. I would rather humble myself, admit to my sin, and put it behind me because once we repent, then we are forgiven, and it is no more. God erases it and does not remind you of it.

How wonderful is the love of God! "For I will forgive their wickedness and will remember their sins no more." (Hebrews 8:12)

It is Satan who wants us to be rebellious, stubborn, self-willed (wanting our own way), and prideful. He twists our thinking into saying because we were hurt, "No one is ever going to tell me what to do again." But all that does is create a prideful and rebellious spirit and draw us away from God. Satan does not want us to go our own way just to get our way. He knows it draws us away from God and away from his blessings. "Pride goes before destruction, a haughty spirit before a fall." (Proverbs 16:18)

He wants to destroy you. Don't fall for his lies and the twisting thoughts in your mind that draw you away from God. "The thief comes only to steal and kill and destroy; I have come that they may have life, and have it to the full." (John 10:10)

The judgment and consequences that happen as a result of sin are our own fault. God gives us instructions found in his Word, and when we obey, we are blessed and protected, but the opposite is true when we disobey and choose our own will over God's. What we sow, we will reap! "Do not be deceived: God cannot be mocked. A man reaps what he sows. Whoever sows to please their flesh, from the flesh will reap destruction; whoever sows to please the Spirit, from the Spirit will reap eternal life. Let us not become weary in doing well, for at the proper time we will reap a harvest if we do not give up. Therefore, as we have the opportunity, let us do good to all people, especially to those who belong to the family of believers." (Galatians 6:7–10)

This is why God says to stay close to Him and why He gives us instructions found in His Word to follow. It is to give us promises and guidelines to follow that will protect us and bless us.

"Blessed is the one who does not walk in step with the wicked or stand in the way that sinners take or sit in the company of mockers, but whose delight is in the Law of the Lord, and who meditates on his Law day and night. That person is like a tree planted by streams of water, which yields its fruit in season and whose leaf does not wither—whatever they do prospers. Not so the wicked! They are like chaff that the wind blows away. Therefore the wicked will not stand in the judgment, nor sinners in the assembly of the righteous. For the Lord watches over the way of the righteous, but the way of the wicked leads to destruction." (Psalms 1)

God wants you to read His Word and stay close to Him in order to guard and protect your heart so evil cannot find its way in. "Above all else, guard your heart, for everything you do flows from it." (Proverbs 4:23)

Living by and in truth not only sets your heart free, but it also keeps it free. "Then you will know the truth, and the truth will set you free." (John 8:32)

Truly get to know Jesus, get to know the truth. "Jesus answered, "I am the way and the truth and the life. No one comes to the Father except through me." (John 14:6)

You will get to know who Jesus is through the Bible—it is his story. Living by and according to the Word of God is to bless you and keep you living a victorious life. Living a holy life is for your protection! "Be holy, because I am holy." (1 Peter 1:16) It keeps the devil out. It keeps Him from having ammunition to use against you.

Having Jesus as your Lord and Savior and the Bible as your guide through life is God's pathway of hope to live a life of victory here on earth while we are waiting to home to heaven. Satan will try to tempt you, to oppress you, and to get you to fall away, but if you stay close to God, you will always win. "With God, we will gain the victory, and He will trample down our enemies." (Psalms 60:12)

God will provide a path, a way out. "These things happened to them as examples and were written down as warnings for us, on whom the culmination of the ages has come. So, if you think you are standing firm, be careful that you don't fall! No temptation has overtaken you except what is common to mankind. And God is faithful; He will not let you be tempted beyond what you can bear. But when you are tempted, He will also provide a way out so that you can endure it. Therefore, my dear friends flee from idolatry." (1 Corinthians 10:11–14)

Satan will try to box you in just as he tried to with the Israelites. He worked through people after the wall was repaired. They started imposing harsh fees on their brethren. The people cried out to God for help, and he heard their cry.

"Yet He took note of their distress when He heard their cry" (Psalms 106:44). Nehemiah corrected them, saying, "What you are doing is not right." He ordered the ones taking advantage to stop and to give the money back that they had unfairly taken. God heard the cry of the people, and He will hear yours too. Just cry out to Him when you are in trouble and life gets overwhelming, and He will help. "Give thanks to the Lord, for He is good; his love endures forever. Let the redeemed of the Lord tell their story—those He redeemed from the hand of the foe, those He gathered from the lands, from east and west, from north and south. Some wandered in desert wastelands, finding no way to a city where they could settle. They were hungry and thirsty, and their lives ebbed away. Then they cried out to the Lord in their trouble, and He delivered them from their distress." (Psalms 107:1–6)

Through Nehemiah's overseeing, the wall was rebuilt and the temple through Ezra. All this was due to God's steadfast and unconditional love for his people. "But you, Lord, are a compassionate and gracious God, slow to anger, abounding in love and faithfulness." (Psalms 86:15)

God initiated the repair of the temple through Cyrus. "This is what the Lord says—your Redeemer, who formed you in the womb: I am the Lord, the Maker of all things, who stretches out the heavens, who spreads out the earth by myself, who foils the signs of false prophets and makes fools of diviners, who overthrows the learning of the wise and turns it into nonsense, who carries out the words of his servants and fulfills the predictions of his messengers, who says of Jerusalem, 'It shall be inhabited,' of the towns of Judah, 'They shall be rebuilt,' and of their ruins, 'I will restore them,' who says to the watery deep, 'Be dry, and I will dry up your streams,' who says of Cyrus, 'He is my shepherd and will accomplish all that I please; He will say of Jerusalem, "Let it be rebuilt," and of the temple, "Let its foundations be laid." (Isaiah 44:24–28)

God initiated the rebuilding of the wall through Nehemiah. He placed the desire in their hearts to accomplish his purpose. "My purpose will stand and I will do all that I please." (Isaiah 46:10)

God's love is unconditional and overwhelming for you as well. We did not ask Him to send Jesus to die in our place—that was his plan, his desire. "He saw that there was no one, He was appalled that there was no one to intervene; so his own arm achieved salvation for Him, and His own righteousness sustained Him." (Isaiah 59:16)

Ask God to open your eyes to see the Cyrus's, Nehemiah's, and Ezra's He has placed in your life. "I, the Lord, have called you in righteousness; I will take hold of your hand. I will keep you and will make you to be a covenant for the people and a light for the Gentiles, to open eyes that are blind, to free captives from prison, and to release from the dungeon those who sit in darkness." (Isaiah 42:6–7)

Our God is a God of love and hope, and with each step you take with

Him, each part of your heart gets healed, and the more you surrender to Him, the more of His hope and love will grow. You will not be able to contain it. This is another part of our preparation for eternity—it is to take as many people with us as we can. "Praise be to the God and Father of our Lord Jesus Christ, the Father of compassion and the God of all comfort, who comforts us in all our troubles so that we can comfort those in any trouble with the comfort we ourselves receive from God. For just as we share abundantly in the sufferings of Christ, so also our comfort abounds through Christ. If we are distressed, it is for your comfort and salvation; if we are comforted, it is for your comfort, which produces in you patient endurance of the same sufferings we suffer. And our hope for you is firm because we know that just as you share in our sufferings, so also you share in our comfort." (2 Corinthians 1:3–7)

In doing so, we destroy Satan's plan to destroy God's creation. "He said to them, 'Go into all the world and preach the gospel to all creation. Whoever believes and is baptized will be saved, but whoever does not believe will be condemned. And these signs will accompany those who believe: In My Name, they will drive out demons; they will speak in new tongues; they will pick up snakes with their hands; and when they drink deadly poison, it will not hurt them at all; they will place their hands on sick people, and they will get well." (Mark 16:15–18)

God restores our hope for a blessed and purpose-filled life, hope for family, and to be a witness, and the best hope of all is the hope we have for our eternal home in heaven.

"Even though we speak like this, dear friends, we are convinced of better things in your case—the things that have to do with salvation. God is not unjust; He will not forget your work and the love you have shown Him as you have helped his people and continue to help them. We want each of you to show this same diligence to the very end, so that what you hope for may be fully realized. We do not want you to become lazy, but to imitate those who through faith and patience inherit what has been promised. When

God made his promise to Abraham, since there was no one greater for Him to swear by, He swore by Himself, saying, "I will surely bless you and give you many descendants." And so after waiting patiently, Abraham received what was promised. People swear by someone greater than themselves, and the oath confirms what is said and puts an end to all arguments. Because God wanted to make the unchanging nature of his purpose very clear to the heirs of what was promised, He confirmed it with an oath. God did this so that, by two unchangeable things in which it is impossible for God to lie, we who have fled to take hold of the hope set before us may be greatly encouraged. We have this hope as an anchor for the soul, firm and secure. It enters the inner sanctuary behind the curtain, where our forerunner, Jesus, has entered on our behalf. He has become a high priest forever, in the order of Melchizedek." (Hebrews 6:9–20)

"We always thank God, the Father of our Lord Jesus Christ, when we pray for you because we have heard of your faith in Christ Jesus and of the love you have for all God's people—the faith and love that spring from the hope stored up for you in heaven and about which you have already heard in the true message of the gospel that has come to you. In the same way, the gospel is bearing fruit and growing throughout the whole world—just as it has been doing among you since the day you heard it and truly understood God's grace." (Colossians 1:3–6)

8

~

Expanding The Path

As your heart heals more and more and you grow into spiritual maturity, God wants you to pass it on to be his hands, feet, and voice to a world in need. That is how the gospel spread in the first place, and you do not need to be a preacher in order to do it—you just need to share your testimony, your experience, and the things God does for you on a daily basis. As you become more and more comfortable and sensitive to the leading of the Holy Spirit, you will sense when He wants you to help someone or speak to or pray for them. The best thing of all to use in witnessing is the Word—the Ten Commandments. The purpose of the Law has always been to draw us to God realizing that we need Him. "Now we know that whatever the law says, it says to those who are under the law so that every mouth may be silenced and the whole world held accountable to God. Therefore no one will be declared righteous in God's sight by the works of the law; rather, through the law we become conscious of our sin." (Romans 3:19–20)

The Ten Commandments speak to our conscience, and whether people believe in God or not, they will not be able to argue the fact that they may have told a lie, stolen, killed, committed adultery, and so on. In witnessing to others, it is the Holy Spirit speaking through you, and He will also give you the words to say. "But the Advocate, the Holy Spirit, whom the Father will send in My name, will teach you all things and will remind you of everything I have said to you." (John 14:26)

The more you let go and let God work through you, the easier and more fulfilling it will be. You will not have to look for people; God will bring them into your path. So fear not, and expand the path!

People may not always listen to a lot of Bible verses when their hearts are not set to follow God, but they will listen to the truth of your experience. Whether or not they follow through and pray with you, the seed will be planted, and it is God who will make it grow. That job belongs to Him! "So neither the one who plants nor the one who waters is anything, but only God, who makes things grow"(1 Corinthians 3:7). Everyone searching for a way out of a pit will listen to your testimony of being in a pit and coming out victoriously. God told Abraham that his descendants would be as numerous as the sand on the seashore. Wow! That is a lot, and we are to help fulfill that promise. "I will surely bless you and make your descendants as numerous as the stars in the sky and as the sand on the seashore. Your descendants will take possession of the cities of their enemies." (Genesis 22:17)

In dealing with so much heartache and depression, it is very hard to think outside yourself, but now that your heart is healed, it is time to shine. "Those who are wise will shine like the brightness of the heavens, and those who lead many to righteousness, like the stars forever and ever." (Daniel 12:3)

It is time to get your mind off yourself! You will find you will be much happier when you stop dwelling on your issues and start being the servant of God you were called to be. Remember Peter? He walked on water as long as he looked at Jesus until he started looking at the surroundings, and then he started to sink. Dwelling on all the bad and the "what about me's" keeps you in the wrong position. Keep God and his ways first, and everything else will fall into place. "But seek first his kingdom and his righteousness, and all these things will be given to you as well." (Matthew. 6:33)

Putting God and others first, seeking to serve and show God's love and witness is not only what we are called to do, but it keeps our hearts humble. "Therefore, as God's chosen people, holy and dearly loved, clothe yourselves with compassion, kindness, humility, gentleness and patience." (Colossians 3:12)

When you do this, you become even more conscious of God's over-whelming love as his Holy Spirit speaks to you, guides you, and speaks through you to others. "In your relationships with one another, have the same mindset as Christ Jesus: Who, being in very nature God, did not consider equality with God something to be used to his own advantage; rather, He made Himself nothing by taking the very nature of a servant, being made in human likeness. And being found in appearance as a man, He humbled Himself by becoming obedient to death—even death on a cross!" (Philippians 2:5–8)

Humility and putting others first will actually increase your joy! "In the same way, you who are younger, submit yourselves to your elders. All of you clothe yourselves with humility toward one another, because, 'God opposes the proud but shows favor to the humble." (1 Peter 5:5) "The meek also shall increase their joy in the Lord, and the poor among men shall rejoice in the Holy One of Israel." (Isaiah 29:19)

Getting your mind off yourself and becoming more aware of the people around you will help you to get rid of that ugly, selfish, and self-centered gene. The more love you show and give away, the more you will receive. "Give and it will be given to you. A good measure, pressed down, shaken together and running over, will be poured into your lap. For with the measure you use, it will be measured to you." (Luke 6:38) This verse is not talking about money, although it can apply. If you read the text before it, it talks about loving your enemies. We were once enemies of the cross, living in sin before receiving Jesus as Lord. It is talking about forgiving and not being judgmental. Here is the text in its entirety:

"But to you who are listening I say: Love your enemies, do good to those who hate you, bless those who curse you, pray for those who mistreat you. If someone slaps you on one cheek, turn to them the other also. If someone takes your coat, do not withhold your shirt from them. Give to everyone who asks you, and if anyone takes what belongs to you, do not demand it back. Do to others as you would have them do to you. If you love those who love you, what credit is that to you? Even sinners love those who love them. And if you do good to those who are good to you, what credit is that to you? Even sinners do that. And if you lend to those from whom you expect repayment, what credit is that to you? Even sinners lend to sinners, expecting to be repaid in full. But love your enemies, do well to them, and lend to them without expecting to get anything back. Then your reward will be great, and you will be children of the Most High because He is kind to the ungrateful and wicked. Be merciful, just as your Father is merciful. Do not judge, and you will not be judged. Do not condemn, and you will not be condemned. Forgive, and you will be forgiven. Give and it will be given to you. A good measure, pressed down, shaken together, and running over, will be poured into your lap. For with the measure you use, it will be measured to you." He also told them this parable: "Can the blind lead the blind? Will they not both fall into a pit? The student is not above the teacher, but everyone who is fully trained will be like their teacher. "Why do you look at the speck of sawdust in your brother's eye and pay no attention to the plank in your own eye? How can you say to your brother, 'Brother, let me take the speck out of your eye,' when you yourself fail to see the plank in your own eye? You hypocrite, first take the plank out of your eye, and then you will see clearly to remove the speck from your brother's eye." (Luke 6:27–42)

The more you get rid of yourself, the more room in your heart. You will have to be filled with the light and fruit of Jesus, who is the sinless Son of God. If you have a pot and put seeds in the bottom and fill it halfway with dirt but then proceed to fill it the rest of the way with rocks and cover it completely with them, will there be any room for the seeds to grow? No! Those rocks are all the bitterness, resentment, anger, pride, rebellion, selfishness, inability to forgive, stubbornness, etc. that fill your heart. And with all that weighing your heart down, no wonder you get depressed. Get rid of it, and allow the fruit room to grow. Those emotions only hurt you and not the ones you are mad at. Jesus dealt with rejection, and He overcame it.

With his Spirit in you, you can as well. He is the Son of God, and yet He left the throne of heaven to come to earth and become a man in order to understand us and to be the atonement for our sins. "Since the children have flesh and blood, He too shared in their humanity so that by His death He might break the power of Him who holds the power of death—that is, the devil—and free those who all their lives were held in slavery by their fear of death. For surely it is not angels He helps, but Abraham's descendants. For this reason, He had to be made like them, fully human in every way, in order that He might become a merciful and faithful high priest in service to God, and that He might make atonement for the sins of the people. Because He Himself suffered when He was tempted, He is able to help those who are being tempted." (Hebrews 2:14–18)

That is truly unselfish, and there is no greater love. "Greater love has no one than this, that He lay down his life for his friends." (John 15:13)

Being a self-centered Christian is not only a contradiction to the heart of being a Christian, but it also makes your relationship with God ugly. It tarnishes the unselfish love God bestows on us. Love is not selfish. It is not held in for yourself—it is meant to be given away.

"If I speak in the tongues of men or of angels, but do not have love, I am only a resounding gong or a clanging cymbal. If I have the gift of prophecy and can fathom all mysteries and all knowledge, and if I have a faith that can move mountains, but do not have love, I am nothing. If I give all I

possess to the poor and give over my body to hardship that I may boast, but do not have love, I gain nothing. Love is patient, love is kind. It does not envy, it does not boast, it is not proud. It does not dishonor others, it is not self-seeking, it is not easily angered, and it keeps no record of wrongs. Love does not delight in evil but rejoices with the truth. It always protects, always trusts, always hopes, and always perseveres. Love never fails. But where there are prophecies, they will cease; where there are tongues, they will be stilled; where there is knowledge, it will pass away. For we know in part and we prophesy in part, but when completeness comes, what is in part disappears. When I was a child, I talked like a child, I thought like a child, I reasoned like a child. When I became a man, I put the ways of childhood behind me. For now, we see only a reflection as in a mirror; then we shall see face to face. Now I know in part; then I shall know fully, even as I am fully known. And now these three remain: faith, hope, and love. But the greatest of these is love." (1 Corinthians 13:1–13)

Expanding the path is not becoming a preacher; it is realizing the wonderful gift God gave to the world and sharing it. It is realizing that behind the rough exterior, some people may have beats a heart that may be hurting as much as you were hurt and opening your eyes to the needs of those around you. Hurting people hurt people. You were not always the perfect loving person to those around you before your heart was healed, and others are no different.

You needed love and understanding, mercy and compassion, and God's help. The hurting people in your life, family and friends, and even strangers who God causes to cross your path need the same. And as God placed people in your life to be his heart, his voice, and his extended hand of love to heal your heart, if He places people in your life who are hurting, then it is your responsibility as a child of God to obey. As God opens your eyes to the needs of those around you, answer the call. "But the Lord said to Samuel, "Do not consider his appearance or his height, for I have rejected Him. The Lord does not look at the things people look at.

People look at the outward appearance, but the Lord looks at the heart." (1 Samuel 16:7)

Sometimes that path may require sharing your testimony. "So do not be ashamed of the testimony about our Lord or of me his prisoner. Rather, join with me in suffering for the gospel, by the power of God." (2 Timothy 1:8)

Other times, it may be a shoulder to cry on or to pray with someone. It means to smile more and to think the best of people instead of the worst. "Do nothing out of selfish ambition or vain conceit. Rather, in humility value others above yourselves." (Philippians 2:3) "Be devoted to one another in love. Honor one another above yourselves." (Romans 12:10) It also means to walk up to someone who looks down and compliment them and to be a friend, to let them know you are there for them if they need someone to talk to or pray with and to let them know they are not alone.

At other times, it may be to give in a special offering as the Lord leads you to do an act of kindness, to pay for someone's meal or groceries. Learn to listen to the Holy Spirit within your heart. If you are not sure it is the Holy Spirit, remember this: the devil does not want you to show love or kindness to anyone, he came "to steal, kill, and destroy," and the Lord came and said, "To give life and life more abundantly." We love because He first loved us. Every good and perfect gift is from above. So if it is an act of love and kindness, then yes, it is from God! Now here is the big one: it is just as important to show love in the mission field God has presently placed you in—your home and your own family.

The newfound love, peace, and joy will abound and overflow from your heart, and it will show. As you show unconditional love to others, it is equally important for you to do the same in your own household—direct and indirect family. What good is it to you if you are all smiles at church and outside the home, but once home, you act like the devil? God sees all and knows the heart. "For your ways are in full view of the Lord, and He examines all your paths." (Proverbs 5:21) "If we had forgotten the name of our God or spread out our hands to a foreign god, would not God have discovered it since He knows the secrets of the heart?" (Psalms 44:21)

Love can melt the hardest of hearts, and if you have an unsaved loved one at home, your constant love and unselfish acts of kindness will speak volumes. Our walk must line up with our talk in and outside the home. It will eventually affect them, and it will be noticed by them whether they admit it or not. "Above all, love each other deeply, because love covers over a multitude of sins." (1 Peter 4:8)

Jesus ate with the sinners, and the Pharisees condemned them. "Therefore, there is now no condemnation for those who are in Christ Jesus, because through Christ Jesus the law of the Spirit who gives life has set you free from the law of sin and death. For what the law was powerless to do because it was weakened by the flesh, God did by sending his own Son in the likeness of sinful flesh to be a sin offering. And so He condemned sin in the flesh, in order that the righteous requirement of the law might be fully met in us, who do not live according to the flesh but according to the Spirit." (Romans 8:1–4)

Love will go before you and reach their hearts. That is what the cross did for all of us. "But God demonstrates His own love for us in this: While we were still sinners, Christ died for us." (Romans 5:8)

The closer you are to God, the more sensitive you will be to the Holy Spirit. To be able to live a victorious life in Christ led by his Spirit and given the strength and ability to love all people unconditionally (which is a huge undertaking), this is very important. We are to live a life of love. This is what tells the world that we are Christians and that there is indeed something different about us. "And now these three remain: faith, hope, and love. But the greatest of these is love" (1 Corinthians 13:13). If not, then how we are any different from the rest of the world, and what will make them want what we have? Someone I once knew told me before He was saved that He noticed a difference in me. And although he was not ready at the time to receive Jesus, he would tell me, "I wish I had the peace that you have."

"If you love those who love you, what reward will you get? Are not even the tax collectors doing that? And if you greet only your own people, what are you doing more than others? Do not even pagans do that?" (Matthew. 5:46–47)

We must learn to be led by the Spirit and listen to his voice within our hearts and not our minds. "So I say, walk by the Spirit, and you will not gratify the desires of the flesh. For the flesh desires what is contrary to the Spirit, and the Spirit what is contrary to the flesh. They are in conflict with each other so you are not to do whatever you want. But if you are led by the Spirit, you are not under the law." (Galatians 5:16–18)

The love that we show will go before us, and the peace that shines from us will tell the world before we even utter a word that there is something different about us. They will want to know why especially if they are going through something difficult and want the peace that we have. This will be an open door for you to share your testimony. The love, joy, and peace that shine from you expand the path as much as the testimony you share. Your words and your actions must agree. The world is watching. Not everyone, especially if they are not saved, will receive Scripture. "The god of this age has blinded the minds of unbelievers so that they cannot see the light of the gospel that displays the glory of Christ, who is the image of God." (2 Corinthians 4:4) But everyone receives, wants, and needs to be loved. Realizing you were a sinner and seeing the overwhelming love of Jesus, who died in your place before you even received Him, melted your heart. That same love will go before you and linger on behind you and will eventually affect those around you who need it.

"But to you who are listening I say: Love your enemies, do good to those

who hate you, bless those who curse you, pray for those who mistreat you. If someone slaps you on one cheek, turn to them the other also. If someone takes your coat, do not withhold your shirt from them. Give to everyone who asks you, and if anyone takes what belongs to you, do not demand it back. Do to others as you would have them do to you. If you love those who love you, what credit is that to you? Even sinners love those who love them. And if you do good to those who are good to you, what credit is that to you? Even sinners do that. And if you lend to those from whom you expect repayment, what credit is that to you? Even sinners lend to sinners, expecting to be repaid in full. But love your enemies, do well to them, and lend to them without expecting to get anything back. Then your reward will be great, and you will be children of the Most High because He is kind to the ungrateful and wicked. Be merciful, just as your Father is merciful. "Do not judge, and you will not be judged? Do not condemn, and you will not be condemned. Forgive, and you will be forgiven. Give and it will be given to you. A good measure, pressed down, shaken together, and running over, will be poured into your lap. For with the measure you use, it will be measured to you." (Luke 6:27–38)

After the temple was rebuilt in Ezra, it states that they put things back in order to worship and give offerings unto the Lord. They set in place the offering and the sacred food, which was the part of the offering that belonged to the priests. "When anyone brings a grain offering to the Lord, their offering is to be of the finest flour. They are to pour olive oil on it, put incense on it, and take it to Aaron's sons the priests." (Leviticus 2:1–2) "He shall take out the memorial portion from the grain offering and burn it on the altar as a food offering, an aroma pleasing to the Lord. The rest of the grain offering belongs to Aaron and his sons; it is a most holy part of the food offerings presented to the Lord." (Leviticus 2:9–10)

Although God does not want legalism but heart, He does not want chaos either. Where there is chaos and everyone going their own way, you will find disorder, and sin follows. "For where you have envy and selfish ambition, there you find disorder and every evil practice." (James 3:16)

This is why He gives us his Book of Instructions—the Bible. Is your life a life of victory or constant chaos? Are you reading the Bible? If not, then that is probably why.

Stubbornness saying "I don't need it" is like saying "No" to a teacher giving an exam and asking if you want it to be an open-book test. The Bible is life to our soul, and He says choose life! "This day I call the heavens and the earth as witnesses against you that I have set before your life and death, blessings and curses. Now choose life, so that you and your children may live and that you may love the Lord your God, listen to his voice, and hold fast to Him. For the Lord is your life, and He will give you many years in the land He swore to give to your fathers, Abraham, Isaac, and Jacob." (Deuteronomy 30:19–20)

Ask yourself, "Is my way working?" Our God is one of order and peace, meaning you know what needs to be done and have a direction to follow. When making any decisions, one way to know if God wants you to do it or not is by peace. "For God is not a God of disorder but of peace—as in all the congregations of the Lord's people." (1 Corinthians 14:33)

If you do not have peace in your heart, then I suggest not doing it and going to the Lord in prayer. "Rejoice in the Lord always. I will say it again: Rejoice! Let your gentleness be evident to all. The Lord is near. Do not be anxious about anything, but in every situation, by prayer and petition, with thanksgiving, present your requests to God. And the peace of God, which transcends all understanding, will guard your hearts and your minds in Christ Jesus." (Philippians 4:4–7)

The Bible is one of the most important ways God uses to direct our steps. "Your Word is a lamp for my feet, a light on my path" (Psalms 119:105)

The priests also had to minister with the Urim and Thummin, which were precious stones used to inquire of the Lord for his direction. They represented light and perfection. Jesus is the Light of the world, and when the light is turned on, the darkness leaves. Everything that was in the dark is now exposed and in view, and walking in the light with the Light of the world within your heart, you will walk in God's perfect will as you follow and trust in Jesus. "Do not conform to the pattern of this world, but be transformed by the renewing of your mind. Then you will be able to test and approve what God's will is—his good, pleasing, and perfect will." (Romans 12:2)

These stones were worn on the breast piece, which is close to your heart where the Lord resides. Part of expanding the path is knowing God's direction, his purpose, and his will for your life. You will never be satisfied in life as long as you live outside of God's will and purpose for your life. "I know that you can do all things; no purpose of yours can be thwarted." (Job 42:2)

Remember Jonah? "When my life was ebbing away, I remembered you, Lord and my prayer rose to you, to your holy temple. 'Those who cling to worthless idols turn away from God's love for them. But I, with shouts of grateful praise, will sacrifice to you. What I have vowed I will make good. I will say, "Salvation comes from the Lord."' And the Lord commanded the fish, and it vomited Jonah onto dry land." (Jonah 2:7–10)

To those who pridefully and stubbornly or even out of fear resist the call of God on their life and continue to go their own way, no matter the reason is still disobedience and idolatry. We are not above God and will not have true joy living apart from Him but will have complete joy in serving Him. "For it is we who are the circumcision—we who worship in the Spirit of God and find our joy in the Messiah Jesus. We have not placed any confidence in the flesh." (Philippians 3:3) An idol is anything you give excessive devotion to or run to for peace. If it is not God, then you have an idol.

Whatever you put first before God is your god, and if you are follow-ing your will instead of God's, then you have and maybe unknowingly set yourself up as an idol above God. Repent and turn back to God. He is always waiting with open arms as the father of the prodigal son. God will not bless your disobedience. He loves you too much. But with an overwhelming flood of grace, mercy, and compassion, He will shower you with love and blessings when you return. "So David went to Baal Perazim, and there he defeated them. He said, 'As waters break out, the Lord has broken out against my enemies before me.' So that place was called Baal Perazim." (2 Samuel 5:20)

He will be your Jehovah Perazim, which means "breakthrough as a flood." In Hebrew, Baal Perazim means "Possessor of breaches," and Breaches mean "A tear or rupture." What happens when you have a tear or a rupture in anything? What was inside floods out! Jehovah Perazim— our breakthrough as a flood! God's blessings and victory breaks out and floods forth into our life.

"If my people, who are called by my Name, will humble themselves and pray and seek my face and turn from their wicked ways, then I will hear from heaven, and I will forgive their sin and will heal their land. Now my eyes will be open and my ears attentive to the prayers offered in this place. I have chosen and consecrated this temple so that my Name may be there forever. My eyes and my heart will always be there. As for you, if you walk before me faithfully as David your father did, and do all I command, and observe my decrees and laws, I will establish your royal throne, as I covenanted with David, your father when I said, 'You shall never fail to have a successor to rule over Israel." (2 Chronicles 7:14–18)

We are God's temple, and a blessed life follows all who obey, receive, and live by the truth, revelations, and will of God. "Where there is no revelation, people cast off restraint; but blessed is the one who heeds wisdom's instruction." (Proverbs 29:18)

But the opposite is true of all who follow after their own way, who choose their own over what they know in their heart what God wants them to do. "You stiff-necked people! Your hearts and ears are still uncircumcised. You are just like your ancestors: you always resist the Holy Spirit!" (Acts 7:51). "Go up to the land flowing with milk and honey. But I will not go with you, because you are a stiff-necked people and I might destroy you on the way." (Exodus 33:3)

Don't wait until God has to "break your stiff neck" so to speak through a trial! "A man who remains stiff-necked after many rebukes will suddenly be destroyed—without remedy." (Proverbs 29:1)

I don't know about you, but I don't like trials. Do not let Satan fool you into thinking by opposing God in any way that he will still bless your disobedience. "The highway of the upright avoids evil; those who guard their ways preserve their lives. Pride goes before destruction, a haughty spirit before a fall. Better to be lowly in spirit along with the oppressed than to share plunder with the proud. Whoever gives heed to instruction prospers, and blessed is the one who trusts in the Lord." (Proverbs 16:17–20)

You may not always understand his path and instructions, but you will be blessed if you obey. "Trust in the Lord with all your heart and lean not on your own understanding; in all your ways submit to Him, and He will make your paths straight." (Proverbs 3:5–6)

We are not called to always understand, but we are called to trust. "See, the enemy is puffed up; his desires are not upright—but the righteous person will live by his faithfulness." (Habakkuk 2:4)

God does so much for us and has already done by dying on the cross, and the beatings He took in our place that a little trust and obedience at times without understanding is not too much to ask. How dare any of us to think or demand otherwise when He endured so much for us. "See, My servant, will act wisely; He will be raised and lifted up and highly exalted. Just as there were many who were appalled at Him—his appearance was so disfigured beyond that of any human being and his form marred beyond human likeness—so He will sprinkle many nations, and kings will shut their mouths because of Him." (Isaiah 52:13–15)

In the beginning, as you obey and follow, you may not always understand, but as you do and walk the path God has led you to, things will become clearer and clearer. It is just like the blind man Jesus healed. He did not receive his sight immediately but little by little.

They came to Bethsaida, and some people brought a blind man and begged Jesus to touch Him. He took the blind man by the hand and led Him outside the village. When He had spit on the man's eyes and put his hands on Him, Jesus asked, "Do you see anything?" He looked up and said, "I see people; they look like trees walking around." Once more Jesus put his hands on the man's eyes. Then his eyes were opened, his sight was restored, and he saw everything clearly." (Mark 8:22–25)

As you learn to obey first and understand last, your faith will grow each time, and you will have confidence in God that "He will never leave you nor forsake you." You will be amazed and overjoyed at the things God will do for you and through you and the provision He has for you when you learn to trust Him completely. "Now to Him who is able to do immeasurably more than all we ask or imagine, according to His power that is at work within us, to Him be glory in the church and in Christ Jesus throughout all generations, forever and ever! Amen." (Ephesians 3:20–21)

Seek God and his way first, and He will take care of the rest and even fix your mess.

"And why do you worry about clothes? See how the flowers of the field grow. They do not labor or spin. Yet I tell you that not even Solomon in all his splendor was dressed like one of these. If that is how God clothes the grass of the field, which is here today and tomorrow is thrown into the fire, will

He not much more clothe you—you of little faith? So do not worry, saying, 'What shall we eat?' or 'What shall we drink?' or 'What shall we wear?' For the pagans run after all these things, and your heavenly Father knows that you need them. But seek first his kingdom and his righteousness, and all these things will be given to you as well. Therefore do not worry about tomorrow, for tomorrow will worry about itself. Each day has enough trouble of its own." (Matthew. 6:28–34)

The result is beautiful, wonderful peace within. "You will keep in perfect peace those whose minds are steadfast because they trust in you." (Isaiah 26:3)

There will come a day when it will be too late to choose God's path and those who sadly enough choose their own way will reject God straight into hell. We must remember that God is love, but He is also just and holy, and the unholy—those who have not received Jesus as Lord and live a life of constant rejection of Him—will not enter into heaven. We may be the only Jesus that some people see, which is why living a life that is a testimony to Jesus and sharing your faith when God places people in your path is so important. Trust God to give you the words to say knowing that if He brought you to something, He will also bring you through it providing all that is needed along the way because it will be for his glory. God is God Almighty, and we are not. He knows what He is doing, just trust Him— trust in his love, and submit to Him and his way. His way always wins, and those in it are blessed! I for one want to be on the winning side! It would tear my heart apart if, on the Day of Judgment, I see a face that crossed my path on earth, along with the opportunity to witness, and I turned away. Then to have to watch them be sent to hell eternally due to their own choice of rejection and no one else bothered to witness either, not even one. Yes, by your own choices, and will you choose your eternal destiny? We are given the choice, and God even says, "Choose life." He wants to bless us, and He wants us with Him.

In Nehemiah, there were gatekeepers, and when it was dark, no one was allowed to enter through the gate. But when the sun rose, the gate was opened. This is a symbol of Jesus, who is the Light of the world. When He came into the world that was dark with sin, the light of his glory illuminated the darkness and sin within the hearts of man. When He rose from the dead, the pathway to salvation was opened. Jesus is the only way; Jesus and not our own, not Muslim, not Buda, not Hindu, or anyone or anything else; only one way—Jesus. "Salvation is found in no one else, for there is no other name under heaven given to mankind by which we must be saved." (Acts 4:12)

"Jesus answered, 'I am the way and the Truth and the Life. No one comes to the Father except through Me." (John 14:6)

There will also come a day when the gate, the doorway to eternal life, will close and we must all make the right choice now before it is too late because not one person here on earth knows the hour and time of their death; only God. "A person's days are determined; you have decreed the number of his months and have set limits He cannot exceed." (Job 14:5)

God wants to bless us and fill our hearts with joy and peace, but He also wants us to remember our life here on earth is short. Eternity is forever. Where will you spend it? This is why we are to be prepared and there to help expand the path. No one knows when their time will come to pass away or when the second coming will happen. It could be tomorrow.

"At that time people will see the Son of Man coming in clouds with great power and glory. And He will send his angels and gather his elect from the four winds, from the ends of the earth to the ends of the heavens. 'Now learn this lesson from the fig tree: As soon as its twigs get tender and its leaves come out, you know that summer is near. Even so, when you see these things happening, you know that it is near, right at the door. Truly I tell you, this generation will certainly not pass away until all these things have happened. Heaven and earth will pass away, but my words will never pass away. But about that day or hour, no one knows, not even the angels in heaven, nor the

Son, but only the Father. Be on guard! Be alert! You do not know when that time will come. It's like a man going away: He leaves his house and puts his servants in charge, each with their assigned task, and tells the one at the door to keep watch. Therefore keep watch because you do not know when the owner of the house will come back—whether in the evening, or at midnight, or when the rooster crows, or at dawn. If He comes suddenly, do not let Him find you sleeping. What I say to you, I say to everyone: 'Watch!" (Mark 13:26-37)

That is also why we are called "to tend the flock" and to be watchmen. We are called to be the heart, hands, feet, and voice of Jesus to the lost. "Follow God's example, therefore, as dearly loved children and walk in the way of love, just as Christ loved us and gave Himself up for us as a fragrant offering and sacrifice to God." (Ephesians 5:1–2)

As God places people in your life and you feel the Holy Spirit tugging at your heart, listen and obey. You are called to be his extended hand of love. He says if we love Him, then we are to obey Him and do unto others what He has done for us—love them. "Again Jesus said, "Simon son of John, do you love me?" He answered, "Yes, Lord, you know that I love you." Jesus said, "Take care of my sheep" (John 21:16). One of his greatest commands, besides loving Him, is to love one another as we love ourselves. If we truly love Him, we will want to obey Him. "And now, dear lady, I am not writing you a new command, but one we have had from the beginning. I ask that we love one another. And this is love: that we walk in obedience to his commands. As you have heard from the beginning, His command is that you walk in love." (2 John 1:5–6)

When we love ourselves and others from the love of God within our hearts, then we will not want to hurt ourselves or others. We will instead want to be a blessing to them. "Let us draw near to God with a sincere heart and with the full assurance that faith brings, having our hearts sprinkled to cleanse us from a guilty conscience and having our bodies washed with pure water. Let us hold unswervingly to the hope we profess, for He who promised is faithful. And let us consider how we may spur one another on toward love and good deeds, not giving up meeting together, as some are in the habit of doing, but encouraging one another— and all the more as you see the Day approaching." (Hebrews 10:22–25)

The Holy Spirit within us fills us with a love of God so great it compels us to share Christ, obey, and worship God and love others.

"Since, then, we know what it is to fear the Lord, we try to persuade others. What we are is plain to God, and I hope it is also plain to your conscience. We are not trying to commend ourselves to you again, but are giving you an opportunity to take pride in us so that you can answer those who take pride in what is seen rather than in what is in the heart. If we are "out of our mind," as some say, it is for God; if we are in our right mind, it is for you. For Christ's love compels us, because we are convinced that one died for all, and therefore all died. And He died for all, that those who live should no longer live for themselves but for Him who died for them and was raised again." (2 Corinthians 5:11–15)

In love, Jesus came to earth to be the atoning sacrifice for our sins; in love, He died for us, and his Spirit within us is still the same today. He does not change.

"Jesus Christ is the same yesterday and today and forever." (Hebrews 13:8)

Part 5: With Dwellings

"With dwellings."

9

～～

Raise Up More Houses

God has an eternal purpose for everything He does. Our life on earth is short, and where we choose to spend eternity will be a decision that will last forever—no going back. As well, the missed opportunities we had on earth to make a difference for God will be forever lost.

If you lose your selfish pride and attitude that is only out to take care of your own issues and forget everyone else's, then you will see God will take care of yours. If you humble yourself— just as Jesus, the Son of God, did for you—you will see that there is overwhelming joy in serving God and not only for you, but it will shine from you, and you will give it away as an effect. "Your love has given me great joy and encouragement, because you, brother, have refreshed the hearts of the Lord's people." (Philemon 1:7)

When the temple was built, Ezra returned to Jerusalem under orders of the king to instruct the people in the law bringing with Him silver and gold for the temple. The silver represents redemption, and the gold represents the deity and glory of God. When your heart is healed and your sweet fellowship with God is restored, you being the temple of God, his glory will shine through you to others. God wants all people to be saved, and His glory that shines through you will draw people to Him due to the love, joy, and peace that you glow. "No one can come to me unless the Father, who sent me draws them, and I will raise them up at the last day." (John 6:44)

They will want to know how they can have it too especially if they are aware of some of the issues going on in your life. God is patient, and He wants hearts to turn to Him rather than have to discipline as a loving Father as to do. "The Lord is not slow in keeping his promise, as some understand slowness. Instead He is patient with you, not wanting anyone to perish, but everyone to come to repentance." (2 Peter 3:9)

God is able to save and call to repentance, and He will use us when we say "Yes" and allow Him to use our mouth, hands, and feet. Two times in chapters 6 and 7 of Ezra, it is stated that God changed the heart and attitude of King Cyrus. God is able to change people's attitudes, and your service helps Him to accomplish this, and it has a two-fold effect—it leads others to Christ, and it builds our own faith each time we are used. In the book of John, when Lazarus died, Jesus could have taken the grave clothes off Lazarus when he called him out from the grave. But instead, He used others, saying, "Jesus said to them, "Take off the grave clothes and let Him go." (John 11:44)

Witnessing is only part, but serving is also part of building the kingdom of God—of raising up more houses. Jesus "Went about doing well."

"God anointed Jesus of Nazareth with the Holy Spirit and power, and how He went around doing good and healing all who were under the power of the devil because God was with Him" (Acts 10:38). "Jesus went throughout Galilee, teaching in their synagogues, proclaiming the good news of the kingdom, and healing every disease and sickness among the people." (Matthew. 4:23)

So are we above Him that the same should not apply? No! Your joy will abound as you get your minds off yourself and put on the same attitude as Jesus Christ. "Therefore if you have any encouragement from being united with Christ, if any comfort from his love, if any common sharing in the Spirit, if any tenderness and compassion, then make my joy complete by being like-minded, having the same love, being one in spirit and of one mind. Do nothing out of selfish ambition or vain conceit. Rather, in humility value others above yourselves, not looking to your own interests but each of you to the interests of the others. In your relationships with one another, have the same mindset as Christ Jesus: who, being in very nature God, did not consider equality with God something to be used to his own advantage; rather, He made Himself nothing by taking the very nature of a servant, being made in human likeness. And being found in appearance as a man, He humbled Himself by becoming obedient to death—even death on a cross!" (Philippians 2:1–8)

Allow the Holy Spirit of Jesus in you to live and come alive and love people through you. Your joy will abound! "And God is able to bless you abundantly, so that in all things at all times, having all that you need, you will abound in every good work." (2 Corinthians 9:8)

To be blessed abundantly is to be made whole in your spirit, mind, emotions, and health—and yes, even in your finances and family. Wouldn't that make you overwhelmingly happy?

As you begin to get out of your comfort zone and serve God through healing, prayer ministry, teaching, encouraging, and being led by the Spirit to serve and help in church, community, and family, you are putting on the same attitude as Christ and following his example. "I have set you an example that you should do as I have done for you." (John 13:15) "To this you were called, because Christ suffered for you, leaving you an example, that you should follow in his steps." (1 Peter 2:21)

God does not want to just save you and then that is it. No, He wants you to have a purpose-filled life, and He wants all men to be saved, healed, encouraged, and set free. "This is good, and pleases God our Savior, who wants all people to be saved and to come to a knowledge of the truth." (1 Timothy 2:3–4)

Give yourself fully to the work of the Lord, and you will experience joy, peace, and contentment of soul like you have never known. "Therefore, my dear brothers and sisters, stand firm. Let nothing move you. Always give yourselves fully to the work of the Lord, because you know that your labor in the Lord is not in vain." (1 Corinthians 15:58)

Nehemiah repopulated the cities surrounding Jerusalem. Once the wall was finished then came the next part: populating the area. Don't worry about what to say and how to do it. If the Lord places something in your heart to do or someone in your life to witness to or pray for or just give an encouraging word, then He will also provide for it. He will provide all the knowledge and resources needed to fulfill His purpose.

"Paul called to be an apostle of Christ Jesus by the will of God, and our brother Sosthenes, to the church of God in Corinth, to those sanctified in Christ Jesus and called to be his holy people, together with all those every-where who call on the name of our Lord Jesus Christ—their Lord and ours: Grace and peace to you from God our Father and the Lord Jesus Christ. I always thank my God for you because of his grace given you in Christ Jesus. For in Him, you have been enriched in every way— with all kinds of speech and with all knowledge—God thus confirming our testimony about Christ among you. Therefore, you do not lack any spiritual gift as you eagerly wait for our Lord Jesus Christ to be revealed. He will also keep you firm to the end so that you will be blameless on the day of our Lord Jesus Christ. God is faithful, who has called you into fellowship with His Son, Jesus Christ our Lord." (1 Corinthians 1:3–9)

You also need a refreshing in your spirit. You have been through a lot, and your heart needs to be renewed. When you clean the house and home of your heart where the Holy Spirit dwells, allow Him to give you a refreshing of the Holy Spirit. It is just like going a while without food, your body becomes weak, but once you eat something, your body gains strength again. When you are weak spiritually due to the issues of life and emotional ups and downs, you need to be renewed in your spirit. If not, the enemy will take advantage, count on it!

"When an impure spirit comes out of a person, it goes through arid places seeking rest and does not find it. Then it says, 'I will return to the house I left.' When it arrives, it finds the house unoccupied, swept clean, and put in order. Then it goes and takes with it seven other spirits more wicked than itself, and they go in and live there. And the final condition of that person is worse than the first. That is how it will be with this wicked generation." (Matthew. 12:43–45)

Rededicating yourself and receiving a fresh filling of the Holy Spirit and, above all, being baptized in the Holy Spirit is like putting up a reinforced wall of security around your heart. "John answered them all, 'I baptize you with water. But one who is more powerful than I will come, the straps of whose sandals I am not worthy to untie. He will baptize you with the Holy Spirit and fire." (Luke 3:16)

In fact, the disciples were commanded not to leave Jerusalem, not to go "About doing well" until they were baptized in the Holy Spirit.

On one occasion, while He was eating with them, He gave them this command: "Do not leave Jerusalem but wait for the gift my Father promised, which you have heard me speak about. For John baptized with water, but in a few days you will be baptized with the Holy Spirit." Then they gathered around Him and asked Him, "Lord, are you at this time going to restore the kingdom to Israel?" He said to them: "It is not for you to know the times or dates the Father has set by His own authority. But you will receive power when the Holy Spirit comes on you, and you will be my witnesses in Jerusalem, and in all Judea and Samaria, and to the ends of the earth." (Acts 1:4–8)

There is only one Spirit, but there is a double portion waiting for all to receive. The first portion is the infilling at conversion. "Because you are his sons, God sent the Spirit of his Son into our hearts, the Spirit, who calls out, 'Abba, and Father." (Galatians 4:6)

The second part being filled to the uttermost and clothed with the power of the Holy Spirit, being baptized in the Holy Spirit completes the double portion. "When they had crossed, Elijah said to Elisha, "Tell me, what I can do for you before I am taken from you? Let me inherit a double portion of your spirit," Elisha replied." (2 Kings 2:9) It fills you with even greater joy! "Instead of your shame you will receive a double portion, and instead of disgrace, you will rejoice in your inheritance. And so you will inherit a double portion in your land, and everlasting joy will be yours." (Isaiah 61:7)

Being baptized in the Holy Spirit completes you and brings the gifts of the Holy Spirit alive in you to work through you to others.

"There are different kinds of gifts, but the same Spirit distributes them. There are different kinds of service, but the same Lord. There are different kinds of working, but in all of them and in everyone it is the same God at work. Now to each one, the manifestation of the Spirit is given for the common good. To one there is given through the Spirit a message of wisdom, to another a message of knowledge by means of the same Spirit, to another faith by the same Spirit, to another gifts of healing by that one Spirit, to another miraculous powers, to another prophecy, to another distinguishing between spirits, to another speaking in different kinds of tongues, and to still another the interpretation of tongues. All these are the work of one and the same Spirit, and He distributes them to each one, just as He determines. Just as a body, though one, has many parts, but all its many parts form one body, so it is with Christ. For we were all baptized by one Spirit so as to form one body—whether Jews or Gentiles, slave or free—and we were all given the one Spirit to drink. Even so, the body is not made up of one part but of

many. Now if the foot should say, "Because I am not a hand, I do not belong to the body," it would not for that reason stop being part of the body. And if the ear should say, "Because I am not an eye, I do not belong to the body," it would not for that reason stop being part of the body. If the whole body were an eye, where would the sense of hearing be? If the whole body were an ear, where would the sense of smell be? But in fact, God has placed the parts in the body, every one of them, just as He wanted them to be. If they were all one part, where would the body be? As it is, there are many parts, but one body. The eye cannot say to the hand, "I don't need you!" And the head cannot say to the feet, "I don't need you!" On the contrary, those parts of the body that seem to be weaker are indispensable, and the parts that we think are less honorable we treat with special honor. And the parts that are unpresentable are treated with special modesty, while our presentable parts need no special treatment. But God has put the body together, giving greater honor to the parts that lacked it, so that there should be no division in the body, but that its parts should have equal concern for each other. If one part suffers, every part suffers with it; if one part is honored, every part rejoices with it. Now you are the body of Christ, and each one of you is a part of it. And God has placed in the church first of all apostles, second prophets, third teachers, then miracles, then gifts of healing, of helping, of guidance, and of different kinds of tongues. Are all apostles? Are all prophets? Are all teachers? Do all work miracles? Do all have gifts of healing? Do all speak in tongues? Do all interpret? Now eagerly desire the greater gifts." (1 Corinthians 12:4–31)

You may not possess every gift, but it will be the one or ones fitting for the purpose in Christ God has for you. "For by the grace given me, I say to every one of you: Do not think of yourself more highly than you ought but rather think of yourself with sober judgment, in accordance with the faith God has distributed to each of you. For just as each of us has one body with many members, and these members do not all have the same function, so in Christ we, though many, form one body, and each member belongs to all the others. We have different gifts, according to the grace given to each of us. If your gift is prophesying, then prophesy in accordance with your faith; if it is serving, then serve; if it is teaching, then teach; if it is to encourage, then give encouragement; if it is giving, then give generously; if it is to lead, do it diligently; if it is to show mercy, do it cheerfully. Love must be sincere. Hate what is evil; cling to what is good. Be devoted to one another in love. Honor one another above your-selves. Never be lacking in zeal, but keep your spiritual fervor, serving the Lord." (Romans 12:3–12)

We are to use the spiritual gifts God gives us through the Holy Spirit for his eternal purpose and glory in order to let his light shine. You do not have to be a preacher; instead, listen to your spirit and obey. Your sensitivity in a certain area will be heightened. For example, you are in a store and you see someone walking with a limp. You will feel the Lord's compassion rise up in you from deep within your heart and feel the Holy Spirit tug at your heart to go up to that person and ask to pray for them. "When Jesus landed and saw a large crowd, He had compassion on them and healed their sick." (Matthew. 14:14)

You may have a desire to teach and offer to help in the Sunday school classes or in your daily life with friends and family or church members, the right words will come to you in order to encourage them. If it is words of Wisdom, you may be praying for someone, and the right verses will come to you to pray over them. If your gift is healing when you pray for a person, they will be healed. It will come easier to you than you expect and will become a part of who you are. You just have to do it.

"One day Peter and John were going up to the temple at the time of prayer— at three in the afternoon. Now a man who was lame from birth was being carried to the temple gate called Beautiful, where he was put every day to beg from those going into the temple courts. When he saw Peter and John about to enter, he asked them for money. Peter looked straight at Him, as did John. Then Peter said, "Look at us!" So the man gave them his attention, expecting to get something from them. Then Peter said, "Silver or gold I do not have, but what I do have I give you. In the name of Jesus Christ of Nazareth, walk." Taking Him by the right hand, He helped Him

up, and instantly the man's feet and ankles became strong. He jumped to his feet and began to walk. Then he went with them into the temple courts, walking and jumping, and praising God. When all the people saw Him walking and praising God, they recognized Him as the same man who used to sit begging at the temple gate called Beautiful, and they were filled with wonder and amazement at what had happened to Him." (Acts 3:1–10)

It will have a domino effect. Those who see will give glory to God along with the one healed and will increase your faith even more. This is raising up more houses, spiritual houses!

Ask and you will receive the baptism, the awakening of the Holy Spirit within you; wait and keep asking, for it is promised. If you do not receive it right away, the very first time you pray and ask, keep asking! It will happen; it is a matter of faith. You receive the infilling of the Holy Spirit by faith and by asking upon salvation.

"So I say to you: Ask and it will be given to you; seek and you will find; knock and the door will be opened to you. For everyone who asks receives; the one who seeks finds; and to the one who knocks, the door will be opened. "Which of you fathers, if your son asks for a fish, will give Him a snake instead? Or if he asks for an egg, will give him a scorpion? If you then, though you are evil, know how to give good gifts to your children, how much more will your Father in heaven give the Holy Spirit to those who ask Him?" (Luke 11:9–13)

The Holy Spirit and the power of the Holy Spirit may be awakened in you in church either by just worshiping or by having the pastor pray over you. Or you may receive it in your own praise and worship time in the quietness of your own home. Ask and then put on some praise music and begin verbally praising and worshiping the Lord. Keep praising Him until the restlessness of your flesh leaves and the sweet peace of God's presence fills your spirit. Then keep praising Him.

The baptism is different in every person, but the evidence is the same, and that is speaking in tongues. The Holy Spirit will start speaking through you in syllables. He will just take over as you keep verbally praising God. It may sound just like gibberish to you but fear not! It is the Holy Spirit! "He said to them, "Go into all the world and preach the gospel to all creation. Whoever believes and is baptized will be saved, but whoever does not believe will be condemned. And these signs will accompany those who believe: In My name, they will drive out demons; they will speak in new tongues; they will pick up snakes with their hands; and when they drink deadly poison, it will not hurt them at all; they will place their hands on sick people, and they will get well." (Mark 16:15–18)

It is truly a wonderful feeling, and the best part is that Satan cannot understand it. He can hear and understand your words but the language of the Holy Spirit He cannot or can He read your mind. This is why it is said to pray in the Spirit on all occasions. "And pray in the Spirit on all occasions with all kinds of prayers and requests. With this in mind, be alert and always keep on praying for all the Lord's people" (Ephesians 6:18). "So what shall I do? I will pray with my spirit, but I will also pray with my understanding; I will sing with my spirit, but I will also sing with my understanding." (1 Corinthians 14:15)

With your words, you can speak with negativity, doubt, and fear and give Satan ammunition to you against you and tempt you, or you can use your words to defeat him. The Holy Spirit is gentle, so there is no need to fear and or to be afraid of how you receive it or if you will. It is promised! And in raising up more houses, it is vital. We need all the Lord can give, all the spiritual power, weapons, and gifts He wants to bless us with and display through us to aid in doing his will and defeat the devil.

If you allow Him, God will use the cracked places in your heart to make a message out of your mess.

"You have enlarged the nation and increased their joy; they rejoice before you as people rejoice at the harvest, as warriors rejoice when dividing the plunder." (Isaiah 9:3)

10

∽

Secure The House

Now I bet you are wondering what about the last three gates. We will discuss them in this chapter. As part of living a victorious life, you need to guard your heart in whatever means you can with all the spiritual gifts the Lord will bestow on you.

"Above all else, guard your heart, for everything you do flows from it." (Proverbs 4:23) It would be nice to be able to live a life free of enemy attacks, but that is not very realistic as long as Satan still roams the earth. "Be alert and of sober mind. Your enemy the devil prowls around like a roaring lion looking for someone to devour." (1 Peter 5:8)

That is why we must guard our hearts with what we listen to, what we watch, what we read, and who we associate with on a daily basis. "Do not be misled: 'Bad company corrupts good character.'" (1 Corinthians 15:33) Satan is not going to sit idly by and allow you to live a victorious life, making a difference for God without trying to get you to turn away from him by temptation or twisting your thoughts to become angry at him.

In Nehemiah, Satan worked through Sanballat to try to make the Israelites afraid and to stop the work. Nehemiah did not fall for it, he stood firm, and we must do the same. "If you do not stand firm in your faith, you will not stand at all." (Isaiah 7:9) Satan will try to intimidate you as he did to Nehemiah and the Israelites. Sanballat tried to get Nehemiah to leave the work and meet with Him some distance away. Again Nehemiah stood firm. Satan will try to make you afraid, condemn you, and make you feel bad about yourself and compromise. This is why you must know the Word of God. Jesus used it in the desert as He was being tempted by the devil. Satan tried to twist the Word and use it against Him. "Then Jesus was led by the Spirit into the wilderness to be tempted by the devil. After fasting for forty days and forty nights, He was hungry. The tempter came to Him and said, "If you are the Son of God, tell these stones to become bread." Jesus answered, "It is written: 'Man shall not live on bread alone, but on every word that comes from the mouth of God." (Matthew. 4:1–4)

Don't you find that kind of humorous? Satan tried to tempt Jesus who is the Word by twisting the Word. Jesus was weak, and when we are weak and weary, that will be the time that Satan will try to come against us and get us to fall away from God. "Watch and pray so that you will not fall into temptation. The spirit is willing, but the flesh is weak." (Matthew. 26:41)

Don't fall for it! Stand firm! You will be delivered! "Do not be afraid. Stand firm and you will see the deliverance the Lord will bring you today. The Egyptians you see today you will never see again." (Exodus 14:13)

You need discernment to recognize Satan's tactics, and you must know the Word of God. It is your weapon and the battle for your victory in life, and your soul is spiritual warfare, and you need spiritual weapons to fight against the enemy. This leads us to the next gate—the Horse Gate. The Horse Gate stands for spiritual warfare. This gate was repaired by the priests, which symbolized Jesus. We cannot face any trials without Jesus

Christ. "I am the vine; you are the branches. If a man remains in Me and Me in him, he will bear much fruit; apart from Me you can do nothing." (John 15:5)

Jesus came in the flesh so He could understand us in our trials and weak moments and have mercy and compassion. "Since the children have flesh and blood, He too shared in their humanity so that by his death He might destroy Him who holds the power of death— that is, the devil." (Hebrews 2:14) His humanity helps Him to understand our weakness and temptations.

"For this reason, He had to be made like his brothers in every way, in order that He might become a merciful and faithful High Priest in service to God, and that He might make atonement for the sins of the people. Because He Himself suffered when He was tempted, He is able to help those who are being tempted." (Hebrews 2:17–18) Jesus was tried and tested, ridiculed and rejected, and crucified. He overcame, and through his Holy Spirit within us, we can as well.

"I have told you these things, so that in me you may have peace. In this world, you will have trouble. "But take heart! I have overcome the world." (John 16:33)

The Horse Gate was near the temple, which represents God and His Word. "In the beginning was the Word, and the Word was with God, and the Word was God. He was with God in the beginning" (John 1:1–2). "The Lord is in his holy temple; the Lord is on his heavenly throne. He observes the sons of men; his eyes examine them." (Psalms 11:4)

God's Word is living and active and is powerful. "The Son is the radiance of God's glory and the exact representation of his being, sustaining all things by his powerful Word." (Hebrews 1:3) "May the praise of God be in their mouths and a double-edged sword in their hands, to inflict vengeance on the nations and punishment on the peoples, to bind the kings with fetters, their nobles with shackles of iron, to carry out the sentence written against them? This is the glory of all His saints." (Psalms 149:6–9)

We cannot fight Satan without God and His Word. "Finally, be strong in the Lord and in His mighty power. Put on the full armor of God so that you can take your stand against the devil's schemes. For our struggle is not against flesh and blood, but against the rulers, against the authorities, against the powers of this dark world, and against the spiritual forces of evil in the heavenly realms. Therefore put on the full armor of God, so that when the day of evil comes, you may be able to stand your ground, and after you have done everything, to stand. Stand firm then, with the belt of truth buckled around your waist, with the breastplate of righteousness in place, and with your feet fitted with the readiness that comes from the gospel of peace. In addition to all this, take up the shield of faith, with which you can extinguish all the flaming arrows of the evil one. Take the helmet of salvation and the sword of the Spirit, which is the Word of God. And pray in the Spirit on all occasions with all kinds of prayers and requests. With this in mind, be alert and always keep on praying for all the saints." (Ephesians 6:10–18)

With Jesus in our hearts and the Word of God in our hearts and our minds, we can do anything! "I can do everything through Him who gives me strength." (Philippians 4:13) Through Jesus and the Word, God will fight our battles for us, and we will win the victory! "With God, we will gain the victory, and He will trample down our enemies." (Psalms 60:12)

Staying close to God and reading his Word daily will help you to keep your heart pure. "Who may ascend the mountain of the Lord? Who may stand in his holy place? The one who has clean hands and a pure heart, who does not trust in an idol or swear by a false god. They will receive blessings from the Lord and vindication from God their Savior." (Psalms 24:3–5)

It is in keeping our hearts pure that we win the battle and do not give Satan any ammunition to use against us and no reason to accuse us of anything. "Once you were alienated from God and were enemies in your minds because of your evil behavior. But now He has reconciled you by Christ's physical body through death to present you holy in his sight, without blemish and free from accusation—if you continue in your faith, established and firm, and do not move from the hope held out in the gospel. This is the gospel that you heard and that has been proclaimed to every creature under heaven, and of which I, Paul, have become a servant." (Colossians 1:21–23)

Keeping our hearts secure in the Lord and a close relationship with Him will also keep us prepared for his return, which leads us to the next gate— the East Gate. The East Gate represents a place of preparation or place of anticipation. We are to be prepared and wait in expectation in everyday life for what God has planned for us. "For I know the plans I have for you, declares the Lord, plans to prosper you and not to harm you, plans to give you hope and a future. Then you will call upon me and come and pray to me, and I will listen to you. You will seek me and find me when you seek me with all your heart. I will be found by you, declares the Lord, and bring you back from captivity." (Jeremiah 29:11–14)

It is also a place more importantly symbolizing the need for continual preparation and expectation for the Lord to come back—the rapture— and take us home. The Lord will come from the East when He comes to take us home. "In the west, people will respect the name of the Lord; in the east, they will glorify Him. For He will come like a raging flood tide driven by the breath of the Lord." (Isaiah 59:19) "For as lightning that comes from the east is visible even in the west, so will be the coming of the Son of Man." (Matthew. 24:27)

The Lord has told us ahead of time that we will all die one day and will either spend it in eternity or hell with the devil, and He gives each of us the choice to decide on our own. No one knows the hour and time of their death or when the Lord will return. "Now, brothers, about times and dates we do not need to write to you, for you know very well that the day of the Lord will come like a thief in the night." (1 Thessalonians 5:1–2)

Life on earth is preparation for where we will spend eternity. Are you ready? "Here I am! I stand at the door and knock. If anyone hears my voice and opens the door, I will come in and eat with Him and He with me." (Revelations 3:20)

God will let things happen if it is for our good to help us see that we need a Savior and receive Him as Lord. "God does all these things to a man— twice, even three times—to turn back his soul from the pit that the light of life may shine on Him." (Job 33:29–30)

He wants everyone with Him, which is why He is patient with every-one and waits as long as possible for everyone to receive Him. "He is patient with you, not wanting anyone to perish, but everyone to come to repentance." (2 Peter 3:9)

Just as in the parable of the ten virgins, some "sleep" or put off salvation because they want to "party. "The problem with that is no one is given the certainty of having a "tomorrow"— be prepared.

"At that time the kingdom of heaven will be like ten virgins who took their lamps and went out to meet the bridegroom. Five of them were foolish and five were wise. The foolish ones took their lamps but did not take any oil with them. The wise, however, took oil in jars along with their lamps. The bridegroom was a long time in coming, and they all became drowsy and fell asleep. At midnight, the cry rang out, 'Here's the bridegroom! Come out to meet Him!' Then all the virgins woke up and trimmed their lamps. The foolish ones said to the wise, 'Give us some of your oil; our lamps are going out.' 'No,' they replied, 'there may not be enough for both us and you. Instead, go to those who sell oil and buy some for yourselves.' But while they

were on their way to buy the oil, the bridegroom arrived. The virgins who were ready went in with Him to the wedding banquet. And the door was shut. Later the others also came. 'Sir! Sir!' they said. 'Open the door for us!' But He replied, 'I tell you the truth, I don't know you.' Therefore keep watch, because you do not know the day or the hour." (Matthew. 25:1–13)

Satan is doomed, and there will be a new heaven and a new earth. "And the devil, who deceived them, was thrown into the lake of burning sulfur, where the beast and the false prophet had been thrown. They will be tormented day and night forever and ever." (Rev. 20:10)

Heaven and earth will be one of peace. There will be no more wars and no more pain. "Then I saw a new heaven and a new earth, for the first heaven and the first earth had passed away, and there was no longer any sea. I saw the Holy City, the new Jerusalem, coming down out of heaven from God, prepared as a bride beautifully dressed for her husband." (Revelations 21:1–2)

The Lord tells us to be prepared. To be clothed with his righteousness so we will be ready. Are you ready?

"Behold, I come like a thief! Blessed is he who stays awake and keeps his clothes with Him, so that he may not go naked and be shamefully exposed."(Revelations 16:15)

We all have this glorious hope of being with Jesus, and Satan is fighting a losing battle. For in Christ, we have won the victory. We have overcome! "Dear friends, now we are children of God, and what will be has not yet been made known. But we know that when He appears we shall be like Him, for we shall see Him as He is." (1 John 3:2)

"So then, let us not be like others, who are asleep, but let us be alert and self-controlled. For those who sleep, sleep at night, and those who get drunk, get drunk at night. But since we belong to the day, let us be self-controlled, putting on faith and love as a breastplate, and the hope of salvation as a helmet. For God did not appoint us to suffer wrath but to receive salvation through our Lord Jesus Christ. He died for us so that, whether we are awake or asleep, we may live together with Him. Therefore encourage one another and build each other up, just as in fact you are doing." (1 Thessalonians 5:6–11)

The last gate is the Inspection Gate or Miphkad Gate, which is a place of accountability or a place of judgment. Miphkad means "Appointed place" and inspection from Hebrew is miphquad meaning "Judgment or accountability." The East Gate, meaning a "Place of preparation," leads us to the last gate, symbolizing the last gate we will go through—the Judgment Gate. Jesus is coming back to get us, and we will all have to give an account of ourselves.

"But I tell you that men will have to give account on the Day of Judgment for every careless word they have spoken. For by your words you will be acquitted, and by your words, you will be condemned" (Matthew. 12:36–37). "So then, each of us will give an account of Himself to God." (Romans 14:12)

Your eternal salvation and where you will spend eternity relies solely on your choice to believe and receive Jesus. One day, you will have to face that decision. It depends on your faith in God and your belief in Jesus Christ and making Him the Lord of your life. No one can make that choice for you. "For we must all appear before the judgment seat of Christ, that each one may receive what is due Him for the things done while in the body, whether good or bad." (2 Corinthians . 5:10)

"Then I saw a great white throne and Him who was seated on it. Earth and sky fled from his presence, and there was no place for them. And I saw the dead, great and small, standing before the throne, and books were opened. Another book was opened, which is the Book of Life. The dead were judged according to what they had done as recorded in the books." (Revelations 20:11–12)

Sanballat continually tried to infiltrate, intimidate, and spread false reports about the Israelites and get them to compromise. Nehemiah stood firm, and that helped the rest of the Israelites to stand firm as well. The work was finished, and if you stand firm in the Lord firmly rooted in his love, you will have a blessed and joy-filled life.

"For this reason, I kneel before the Father, from whom every family in heaven and on earth derives its name. I pray that out of his glorious riches, He may strengthen you with power through his Spirit in your inner being, so that Christ may dwell in your hearts through faith. And I pray that you, being rooted and established in love, may have power, together with all the Lord's holy people, to grasp how wide and long and high and deep is the love of Christ, and to know this love that surpasses knowledge—that you may be filled to the measure of all the fullness of God. Now to Him who is able to do immeasurably more than all we ask or imagine, according to His power that is at work within us, to Him be glory in the church and in Christ Jesus throughout all generations, forever and ever! Amen." (Ephesians 3:14–21)

In standing firm—rooted in his love and allowing Him to fulfill his purpose through you—not only will joy abound in your heart here on earth, but on that day, when you get to heaven, you will hear Him say, "Well done." And I don't know about you, but standing in his presence alone will make my heart melt. But to hear Him say, "Well done," in the light of his glory and love, I will not be able to do anything but bow in humility. He did so much more for us.

"His master replied, 'Well done, good and faithful servant! You have been faithful with a few things; I will put you in charge of many things. Come and share your master's happiness!" (Matthew 25:23)

Final Thoughts

I hope through the Scriptures and topics found in this book, the Holy Spirit has enlightened you to the path you need to take to receive healing for your broken heart and restore the joy of the Lord. Follow the path and direction the Holy Spirit enlightens you to take. For some of you, the extent of your pain may go so deep that you will need a licensed counselor and psychologist who is experienced in walking you through the painful events that damaged your heart. Learning to release the events and the people who broke your heart to God and forgiving is vital to your healing.

Forgiving will not let them off the hook. God is just, and everyone will reap what they have sown. Forgiving will help you; and holding onto bitterness, resentment, anger, and the inability to forgive does not hurt the other person. They have probably gone on with their life. Holding on to those emotions will keep your heart heavy, sad, and in bondage to pain—it only hurts you. You may say what they did is unforgivable and I have the right to be angry. Well, our Heavenly Father can say that about all of us. "For we all fall short of the glory of God."

While you may have the right to be angry, is it helping you? Is it beneficial to you? Is it getting you out of your pit of darkness? "I have the right to do anything, "you say— but not everything is beneficial. "I have the right to do anything"— but not everything is constructive." (1 Corinthians 10:23) We can do anything through Him who gives us strength. By the Holy Spirit within, you can forgive. He will help you if you ask. Holding onto it creates a wall that you cannot get past until you tear it down by letting go and forgiving.

Only Jesus can you forgive what and who seems unforgivable. He was beaten beyond human recognition, and if that was not enough, tired and worn out from that, He had to carry the cross in which the whole cross weighed close to three hundred pounds and the crossbeam (which is the point that was laid across his shoulders to carry) weighed about one hundred pounds up the hill to Golgotha—Calvary. Jesus is the sinless Son of God, and He came to pay the price for our sins. "His Son paid the price to free us, which means that our sins are forgiven." (Colossians 1:14)

He forgives all our sins upon asking, so who are we to hold back forgiveness? On our own, we can do nothing. "I am the vine; you are the branches. If you remain in me and me in you, you will bear much fruit; apart from me you can do nothing." (John 15:5)

But through Him and his strength, we can do anything, and if you ask, He will help you to forgive. "I can do everything through Christ who gives me strength." (Philippians 4:13)

It is only through Jesus Christ that we are saved and only through Jesus that we can enter into a life of victory and able to overcome any obstacle and any heartache. "I am the Gate; whoever enters through me will be saved." (John 10:8)

He was made flesh so that He could understand our weaknesses. "Since the children have flesh and blood, He too shared in their humanity so that by his death He might break the power of Him who holds the power of death—that is, the devil—and free those who all their lives were held in slavery by their fear of death. For surely it is not angels He helps, but Abraham's descendants. For this reason, He had to be made like them, fully human in every way, in order that He might become a merciful and faithful high priest in service to God, and that He might make atonement for the sins of the people. Because He Himself suffered when He was tempted, He is able to help those who are being tempted." (Hebrews 2:14–18)

It is because of that and through the tests and trials that He went through and over-came, as we place our faith in Him and receive Him into our hearts that we too can overcome. "I have told you these things, so that in me you may have peace. In this world you will have trouble. But take heart! I have overcome the world." (John 16:33)

The process of becoming totally healed is, first of all, to be sure of your salvation, to repent, and to ask for forgiveness. Ask the Lord into your heart, or if saved, rededicate yourself. Next, revisit each painful event and each person who hurt you and release them to God; forgiving and letting go. The next step is to receive a fresh filling of the Holy Spirit and to be baptized in the Holy Spirit. Continue to read the Bible, learn the promises of God in it, and speak them, pray them, and stand on them. "I will bow down toward your holy temple and will praise your Name for your unfailing love and your faithfulness, for you have exalted above all things your Name and your Word." (Psalms 138:2)

The next step is to expand the path, share your testimony, and witness. The next is to raise up more houses by using the gifts of the Holy Spirit. The next is to keep your heart secure, to guard the treasure of your heart where the Holy Spirit resides. Trials will come in life, but as long as you stay close to God and his Word, you will be victorious through every trial, and you will have the continual peace of God within your heart knowing that when trials do come, they will be for God's eternal purpose and will work out for your good.

"We do not want you to be uninformed, brothers and sisters, about the troubles we experienced in the province of Asia. We were under great pressure, far beyond our ability to endure, so that we despaired of life itself. Indeed, we felt we had received the sentence of death. But this happened that we might not rely on ourselves but on God, who raises the dead. He has delivered us from such a deadly peril, and He will deliver us again. On Him, we have set our hope that He will continue to deliver us, as you help us by your prayers. Then many will give thanks on our behalf for the gracious favor granted us in answer to the prayers of many." (2 Corinthians 1:8–11)

Trust God to lead you safely through life; allow Him to heal your heart his way. You will be completely healed and the pain never return, and God's everlasting joy will replace the pain.

"The Spirit of the Sovereign Lord is on Me because the Lord has anointed Me to proclaim good news to the poor. He has sent me to bind up the brokenhearted, to proclaim freedom for the captives and release from darkness for the prisoners, to proclaim the year of the Lord's favor and the day of vengeance of our God, to comfort all who mourn, and provide for those who grieve in Zion—to bestow on them a crown of beauty instead of ashes, the oil of joy instead of mourning, and a garment of praise instead of a spirit of despair. They will be called oaks of righteousness, a planting of the Lord for the display of his splendor." (Isaiah 61:1–3)

Special Invitation

I cannot close this book without giving you the awesome privilege of becoming a child of God, a chance to have every wrong made right and every sin washed away. If you have never asked Jesus into your heart, or maybe you did but you were never sincere, please pray the prayer on the pages following. It will be the best thing you have ever done. After you do this, find a good Church to go to if you do not have one already. Fellowshipping with other Christians will help you on your new walk in Christ. It is also a place to worship God and learn more about Him. Also, tell someone! You must confess! This should be the happiest day of your life because you now know that your eternal home is in heaven! I think that is the best life insurance anyone can have, and it is free! (Romans 10:9-10) "That if you confess with your mouth, 'Jesus is Lord,' and believe in your heart that God raised Him from the dead, you will be saved. For it is with your heart that you believe and are justified, and it is with your mouth that you confess and are saved."

Congratulations and welcome to the family of God!

God Loves You!

(Jeremiah. 31:3) "I have loved you with an everlasting love; I have drawn you with loving-kindness."

I Timothy 2:3-4 "God our Savior, who wants all men to be saved and to come to the knowledge of the truth."

He will not knock on the door of your heart forever. Will you let Him in?

Revelation 3:20 "Here I am! I stand at the door and knock. If anyone hears My voice and opens the door, I will come in and eat with him, and he with Me."

Jesus is the only way to God.
John 14:6 "I am the way, the truth, and the life. No one comes to the Father except through Me."

John 3:3 "I tell you the truth, no one can see the kingdom of God unless he is born again."

And you must make Him Lord of your life.
Matthew 6:24 "No one can serve two masters."
Matthew 7:21 "Not everyone who says to Me, 'Lord, Lord', will enter the kingdom of heaven, but only he who does the will of My Father who is in heaven."

We must leave our old ways behind.
Mark 3:25 "If a house is divided against itself, that house cannot stand."

You can't live according to the flesh and desires of the sinful nature and expect

to have Jesus in your heart. He is holy. He is love. Love and Hate cannot exist together.

Ephesians 4:22-24 "You were taught, with regard to your former way of life, to put off your old self, which is being corrupted by its deceitful desires; to be made new in the attitude of your minds; and to put on the new self, created to be like God in true righteousness and holiness."

God gives you the ability to do His will. He knows it is hard.
Philippians 4:13 "I can do everything through Him who gives me strength."

Romans 3:23 "For all have sinned and fall short of the glory of God."

I John 1:9 "If we confess our sins, He is faithful and just and will forgive us our sins and purify us from all unrighteousness."

John 1:12 "Yet to all who received Him, to those who believed in His name, He gave the right to become children of God."

Romans 10:10 "For it is with your heart that you believe and are justified, and it is with your mouth that you confess and are saved."

Then after you confess and ask forgiveness and receive Jesus into your heart, you must testify (tell someone) and be baptized. In this, God is glorified, and others might be saved by your example.

II Timothy 1:8 "So do not be ashamed to testify about our Lord"

I Peter 3:21 "And this water symbolizes baptism that now saves you also-not the removal of dirt from the body but the pledge of a good conscience toward God. It saves you by the resurrection of Jesus Christ."

Invitation To Salvation Prayer

Dear Almighty Father in heaven, I know that I am a sinner and I ask your forgiveness of all my sins. I want to make You the Lord of my life and I want to serve You all the days of my life. I believe that Jesus Christ died on the cross for my sins. Thank you so much for loving me, and waiting on me to come to the knowledge of the truth! Thank you for my salvation. Please help me and guide me in learning your Word so I can be a light to the world. Please, Jesus, come into my heart, and baptize me with your Holy Spirit. I thank You and praise Your Holy Name and ask all this in the name of Jesus Christ our Lord. Amen.

Other Books By Sandra Lott

Adult Books

Jeremy's Journey
Safe In Papa's Hands
Her Final Curtain
Deep Waters Within
Deep Waters Rage: Sequel to Deep Waters Within
The Train Ride: One Woman's Journey
My Father's Eyes: Seeing Yourself Through The Eyes of Love
Hannah: From Barren to Blossom
Ride the Wind
An Eagle's Flight
A Princess in Waiting
The Princess in the Harlot
God's Love
Step By Step Into A Deeper Walk In Christ
I'm Saved! Where Do I Go From Here?
The Day Hope Was Born: God's Gift of Love
The Holy Spirit & The Baptism of the Holy Spirit
Repairing Broken Walls: Restoring Joy & Peace-The Study Guide
Jewels From the Word & Manna For the Soul
Captivated By God's Love: Poems From the Heart
You've Got This: Learning To Let Go
I'm Saved! What Next? Beginning Your Walk In Christ
Abide in Me: A Seven-Week Study of the Blessings of Being in God's Presence

Children's Books

The Sheep That Went Astray
Naomi's Joy
Molly's Journey to Forgiveness
Tim & Gerald Ray Series: The Wind Has a Voice
Tim & Gerald Ray Series: How Did He Get in There?
Tim & Gerald Ray Series: A Light in the Sky
Tim & Gerald Ray Series: Let's Go Swimming
Tim & Gerald Ray Series: Blowing in the Wind
Tim & Gerald Ray Series: Summer on Grandma's Farm

Sandra Lott was born and raised in San Antonio, Texas, with one sister and two brothers. Sandra loves the mountains, making candles, and jewelry. She is the author of Jeremy's Journey, Deep Waters Within, A Princess in Waiting, Ride the Wind, and more. She has also written children's such as, The Wind Has a Voice and How Did He Get in There, Molly's Journey to Forgiveness, and more. She has written over 34 books to date and began writing poetry as soon as she was saved in June 1998. The Lord gave her, her first book to write right after her son was killed. Writing was not something she sought out. She poured her heart into time spent with the Lord in order to allow Him to heal her heart and the name of her first book was birthed in her spirit along with the chapters and what it was to be about during a devotion time. It was called: God's Love; ironically enough, with all that she was going through, God's love was exactly what she needed.

She is passionate about studying the Bible. She has taught Sunday school, and Bible Study Groups, and has been actively serving in her present church, served in the Celebrate Recovery Ministry, and Homeless Outreach. Sandra was also interviewed on radio shows such as Golden Life Living and WMAP Radio (World's Most Amazing People based out of New York), the Bill Martinez show and a Fox Radio show called the Kim Kennedy Show.

She is a devoted mother of 2 sons (Tim & Gerald Ray), Gerald Ray the youngest, has gone on to be with the Lord due to a car accident. Through the death of her youngest son at the age of 16, a rocky marriage to an alcoholic and the abuse that came with that, and other overwhelming trials, she has drawn close to the loving arms of the Father. Experiencing God's unconditional love as He held her heart in His hands, has created a passion in her to help others grow in their understanding of and receive God's love and grow spiritually. She has the heart to help hurting women discover the princess in Christ that they truly are and overcome abuse. She teaches on topics to help you reach spiritual maturity, persevere through the hard times, and how to reach your destiny in Christ!

Milton Keynes UK
Ingram Content Group UK Ltd.
UKHW020928231123
433129UK00016B/902